P9-DBK-957

KARATE

KARATE

Sanette Smit

THE LYONS PRESS

Guilford, Connecticut

An Imprint of the Globe Pequot Press

First Lyons Press edition 2001

Copyright © 2001 New Holland Publishers (UK) Ltd
Copyright © 2001 in text: Sanette Smit
Copyright © 2001 in illustrations:
New Holland Publishers (UK) Ltd
Copyright © 2001 in photographs: Pieter Smit, with the exception of the
individual photographers and/or their agents as listed on page 96.

First published by New Holland Publishers (UK) Ltd, 2001

ALL RIGHTS RESERVED. No part of this publication may be reproduced
or transmitted in any form or by any means, electronic or mechanical,
including photocopying and recording, or by any information storage
and retrieval system, except as may be expressly permitted by the
1976 Copyright Act or in writing from the publisher.
Requests for permission should be addressed to:
The Globe Pequot Press, P.O. Box 480, Guilford CT 06437.

ISBN 1 58574 380 1

2 4 6 8 10 9 7 5 3 1

Reproduction by Hirt & Carter (Cape) Pty Ltd
Printed and bound in Malaysia by Times Offset (M) Sdn Bhd

DISCLAIMER
While all care has been taken to ensure the
information in this book is correct at the
time of publication, the author and publisher accept no liability for accident, injury, or
any other misadventure incurred in relying
on this book.

AUTHOR'S ACKNOWLEDGEMENTS

I would like to thank principal photographer Pieter Smit and all the other individuals who contributed to this project, among them, Imtiaz Abdulla, Leon Beech, Herman Bosman, Chris Botha, Mark Cosmos, Allen Fourie, Florence Harding, Wendy Jansen, Karen Johnson, Jeffrey Jackson, Nazeem Larney, Wendy Lloyd, Darlene Lubbe, Shane Lucas, Hoosain Narker, Margaret Neethling, Llewellyn Rhoda, Selwyn Rhoda, Johan Roux, Chrislene Smith, Bruce van Rensburg, Nicholas van Schalkwyk, Jody Young, and the students of Funakoshi Karate SA Dojo, Cape Town.

CONTENTS

I NTRODUCTION

Karate originated in the East and was developed as a martial art for use in combat. The word 'karate' derives from Japanese, meaning 'empty hand', implying 'empty of all evil intention'. Today, karate is a means of fighting without weapons. The feet, hands, fingertips, knees and elbows all serve as the natural instruments of attack and self-defence in this, one of the world's most popular martial arts.

Karate is one of the most refined of the martial arts and is characterized by the stylized, controlled and creative performance of techniques, and the agility and strength of the body.

What does karate offer?

Not only is karate an excellent form of self-defence, it also offers the devotee an opportunity to adopt a healthy and balanced way of living — uniting body, mind and spirit. As a sport and martial art, it encourages self-discipline and is a pathway to developing the powers of concentration and awareness. While Karate training is very disciplined, the interactive nature of the sport offers a platform for participants to learn and practise life skills such as humility, mutual respect, sincerity and positive attitude. These, together with integrity — a code of behaviour that includes self-control — form the maxims on which karate is based.

above DOJO TRAINING STIMULATES PROGRESS IN THE INDIVIDUAL AND FACILITATES INTERACTIVE TRAINING IN A GROUP.

opposite THE STANCE FOR WIND-UP POSITIONS, SUCH AS FOR THE THRUST KICK, IS DETERMINED BY ARM AND LEG PLACEMENT.

Many parents encourage their children to participate in a sport that is both fun and exhilarating, because they consider karate discipline training and recognize the sport's potential as character and confidence builder. Karate also helps mould the physique: it tones the body, builds muscle power, promotes flexibility, increases endurance and heightens the overall physical aptitude of the body.

Some people start karate training because they consider mastering the movements a creative challenge. They see the karate — and the training it demands — as a philosophy that adds both meaning and substance to their lives. Karate affords students the opportunity to reflect upon themselves, and their beliefs, attitudes, and behaviour.

Karate caters for both sexes and all age groups (from the age of five up) and has become increasingly popular both as a recreational and competitive sport. The attraction may well lie in the fact that participants have the opportunity to enjoy and take part in an activity that is suitable not only for the individual, but also for competitive performance.

GICHIN FUNAKOSHI BELIEVED THAT TO SUBDUE THE ENEMY WITHOUT FIGHTING WAS THE GREATEST SKILL.

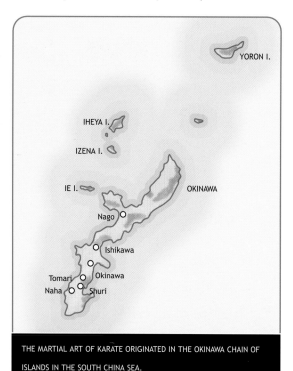

THE MARTIAL ART OF KARATE ORIGINATED IN THE OKINAWA CHAIN OF ISLANDS IN THE SOUTH CHINA SEA.

A short history

Karate dates back more than a thousand years and probably originated from the martial arts of China. Chinese fighting (*kempo*) was imported into Okinawa, a chain of islands under the feudal control of China, situated between Japan and Taiwan in the East China Sea. As the use of weapons was banned in Okinawa around 1470 (and again in 1609), 'empty hand' self-defence became the accepted method of combat.

Gichin Funakoshi, a teacher by profession, was a student of the Okinawan karate masters Yasutsune Itosu and Yasutsune Azato. In 1922, Funakoshi was invited by the Japanese Ministry of Education to give a karate demonstration in Tokyo. The Japanese were so impressed that Funakoshi remained in Tokyo and taught karate at various universities. Two years later, Keio University founded its first karate *dojo*.

Funakoshi was born in 1868 in the royal Okinawan capital of Shuri, and died in 1957, having devoted much of his life to the development of karate.

Understanding the philosophy

General opinion among karate practitioners is that if the *karateka* (practitioner of karate) can abide strictly by the maxims of karate — etiquette, effort, sincerity, self-control, patience and character — then there is no reason why he or she should not live their entire lives according to those very same rules. If *dojo* rules require students to practise good hygiene, refrain from drinking and smoking, be humble and maintain a high standard of discipline, then these principles will naturally become a part of their lives.

Psychological principles

By adopting a positive state of mind in your training, progress may be easier. A positive attitude enhances confidence in the ability to perform, and may make it easier to recognize how to deal with or adapt to any situation, be it in a competitive arena or life in general.

It is more than often the attitude and state of the mind that decides the outcome of any battle.

Principles to work towards

A well-trained *karateka* will develop inner power and balance, and learn both benevolence and compassion. The *karateka* constantly works towards taking the appropriate action in any given situation, and always with courtesy. Devotion and loyalty, truthfulness and sincerity form the very foundation of karate. The great challenge for the individual is to maintain self-control in the face of any event.

SOUND TRAINING DEVELOPS NOT ONLY THE BODY, BUT ALSO THE POWER OF THE MIND.

The various styles

While Funakoshi is recognized as the father of modern karate, other schools developed and sent their teachers to Japan for instruction. As a result, karate slowly became an integral part of the Japanese culture, developing a number of individual styles (*Ryu*).

Apart from the Japanese styles, other forms developed in other countries and had considerable impact on the sport worldwide. Isshin-Ryu was founded by Ticky Donovan, former British champion, and was based on his training in Shotokan, Wado-Ryu and Kyokushinkai. Uechi-Ryu — known for its tough conditioning exercises and the toe-tipped kick targeted to the navel area — is the Okinawan name for the Chinese system Pan Gai Noon founded by Kanbun Uechi.

There are a great many different styles or systems of karate, with four mainstream Japanese styles.

Shotokan

Shoto was the pen name used by Gichin Funakoshi and the term Shotokan means 'Shoto's house or hall'. In this style of karate, emphasis is placed on *kata* training (a fixed sequence of exercises performed without a partner), which makes use of low, strong stances to ensure a solid foundation for the basic techniques. The style is well suited for competition as well as self-defence, and fosters a strong, determined spirit.

In 1957, the Japan Karate Association (JKA), which practices the Shotokan style, was formed with Sensei Masatoshi Nakayama — one of Gichin Funakoshi's top students — as chief instructor. The JKA has continued to develop karate worldwide and has been instrumental in promoting it as a sport.

Goju-Ryu

Goju-Ryu, which means 'hard-soft' style, is a combination of soft Chinese techniques and hard Okinawan methods. This school was founded by Chojun Miyagi (1888—1953). In *kata*, Goju-Ryu emphasizes fast and slow movements, tension and relaxation, with deep abdominal breath-control, and is characterized by small, tight body movements of the body.

top THE SHOTOKAN EMPHASISES *KATA* TRAINING.

above THE EMPHASIS OF GOJU-RYU IS ON HARD AND SOFT METHODS.

Wado-Ryu

Wado-Ryu, which means 'way of harmony', was founded in 1939 by Hironori Otsuka, another of Funakoshi's students. This style of karate uses tension-free techniques (snapping) — participants depend on speed for their power.

Wado-Ryu makes great use of two-man sparring drills developed by Otsuka. The stances are slightly higher than those used in Shotokan, but lower than those used in the Shukokai-style.

Shito-Ryu

In 1928, Kenwa Mabuni founded the Shito-Ryu style (originally termed Hanko-Ryu by Mabuni). Although popular in Japan, it did not however spread much further afield.

A branch style of Shito-Ryu, Shukokai ('way for all') was established in 1950 by Chojiro Tani, who first practiced Shito-Ryu under Sensei Kenwa Mabuni. Sensei Shigeru Kimura, the senior technical instructor outside Japan, developed the style further in the West.

This is a fast style, using high, shortened stances that are designed for natural movement and greater mobility, rather than power.

Respect for all styles

The introspective principles fostered by the martial arts are universal and although there are a great many different karate styles, all have a valid contribution. No particular style is superior to another. What is important is that the *karateka* practising a particular style is committed to training and works towards the betterment of the self. There are many different routes, but the spiritual and physical destination remain the same.

The challenge

The aspiration of every beginner is black-belt status (1st dan), which for many symbolizes power and strength. For the karate devotee, the black belt means recognition, reward and a personal and public acknowledgement of achievement.

top WADO-RYU PRACTITIONERS RELY ON SPEED IN THEIR MOVEMENTS.

above THE SHITO-RYU IS MOST POPULAR IN JAPAN.

STARTING OUT

The sight of karate students parading in their training clothes and the vibrant array of different coloured belts has planted the seeds of curiosity — and even awe — in the mind of many aspiring sportspeople. It is this that has motivated many would-be students to find out more about the martial arts and the sport of karate in particular.

Committing yourself

Karate demands a series of commitments:

- to a particular style based on an understanding of the various options available
- to a particular school that offers convenient and suitable training and changing facilities, and affiliation to national karate governing bodies
- to the teachings of the instructor (*Sensei*), based on their credentials and the quality of instruction
- to all regulations in the *dojo* (place of training)
- to respect the *gi* (attire) and wear it with pride
- to train on the formal and informal 'stage'
- to practise the physical and psychological skills of the sport to perfection
- to oneself.

A new routine

Starting out demands a new routine. Getting used to a new way of life requires an entirely new set of rules:

- adopting a healthier lifestyle: balanced diet, sufficient rest, and abstaining from bad habits such as smoking
- conditioning the body by raising fitness levels
- following a training programme that requires commitment, discipline and sacrifice
- having the ability to persevere against all odds.

The rewards

- Increased self-esteem and maturity.
- Enhanced physique.
- The setting and attaining of goals.

Remember that starting out is just the first step!

above STUDENTS LEARN THAT TRAINING SESSIONS EXTEND BEYOND THE WALLS OF THE DOJO.

opposite PROGRESS FROM WHITE TO BLACK BELT IS A DEMANDING BUT REWARDING PROCESS.

Choosing a school

Not all karate schools follow the same style of karate or even offer the style suggested in the name of the school. A student may, for example, practise the Shotokan style of karate at the Warrior School of Karate. Some schools focus on power training and fighting skills (sport karate), while others lean towards *kata* training (traditional karate training).

To gain a better understanding of the approach and the variation between the different styles of karate being taught, it would be a good idea for you, as the aspirant student, to visit several karate schools in order to:

■ make a comparative study of what the different schools have to offer in terms of training facilities and the like

■ gain an insight and feel for the style of karate that suits your personal needs

■ recognize and relate to a *Sensei's* (instructors) style — be it friendly/disciplined or stark/authoritarian

■ identify a school that instills comfort rather than anxiety.

The search is on

in order to find the right school in a particular area, establish which are registered or affiliated to recognized karate bodies — very important if you intend competing nationally, and especially at an international level.

What to wear

You train barefooted, wearing a karate *gi* (long, white training pants and a loose-fitting jacket). The white (beginner) belt will be included as part of the first suit you buy, and you will need a different colour as you reach the next level in some styles.

Once you have progressed further, you will also need hand mitts and mouthguards to protect your hands and mouth. Although karate is extremely controlled, a split-second error in judgement could result in unexpected contact — and even serious injury. While some schools require their students to wear foot-pads for sparring, it is not compulsory in all *dojos*.

above THE NOVICE KARATEKA, OR KARATE STUDENT, WILL TRAIN BARE FOOT IN A WHITE GI AND A WHITE BELT.

opposite THE MOST BASIC PREMISE ON WHICH KARATE IS BUILT IS MUTUAL RESPECT, INDICATED BEFORE A BOUT WITH A TRADITIONAL BOW.

inset AS KARATEKA GAIN EXPERIENCE AND ENCOUNTER BODY CONTACT WITH AN OPPONENT IN THE ARENA, THEY MAY BE REQUIRED TO WEAR PROTECTIVE GEAR SUCH AS HAND MITTS.

The *Sensei*

Sensei literally means 'first born' (in other words, someone 'born before you in the style'), and is the term used to address the instructor of the class, a position earned through years of hard training and deserving of acknowledgement and respect. Some styles only recognize the title of *Sensei* from 3rd dan — which usually demands some eight years of training.

Before individual interaction with a *Sensei* and before commencing a training session, it is customary for the pupil or class to bow to the *Sensei*. This gesture is repeated at the end of the training session. Apart from being a simple sign of respect, the symbolism behind the gesture represents 'asking to be taught and thanking for being taught'.

The *Sensei* plays a major role in the training and development of the student. It is important to trust the judgment of the *Sensei*, even though the instruction and discipline may appear somewhat harsh at times. Remember that the *Sensei* is guided by years of experience and the knowledge of what really is 'best for you'!

The *dojo*

Karate is practised in a *dojo*, which means 'the place of the way' and refers to the place of learning. This could be a training hall equipped with mirrors and punching bags or an appropriately furnished clubhouse.

But '*dojo*' has a broader meaning — it is a place where devotees share their training and knowledge.

Basic dojo rules

All dojos have a set of regulations that assist with the training regime and the discipline of the students.

- Bowing on entering and leaving the dojo is a sign of respect for the training area, the *Sensei* and other students in the class.
- Shoes should be removed before stepping onto the training area (this is not applicable to all dojos).
- All jewellery should be removed before the commencement of training.
- No alcohol may be consumed before the class.
- No smoking or chewing gum while training.
- Observance of strict rules of hygiene.
- No foul language or bad behaviour will be tolerated.

The correct approach

Karate is the performance of a series of techniques and manoeuvres, and the skill and accuracy with which they are executed lies in the correct approach. From the outset, students are instructed to perform basic techniques — from assuming the correct stance to the execution of blocks, punches, strikes and kicks — with a great measure of precision, strength and patience. It is very important to develop a clear understanding of what is being done and why it is being done in a particular way. Basic methodical training should never be rushed as speed and power training can only be developed from a strong and stable foundation.

Remember, what cannot be achieved today can be achieved tomorrow. The strength of technique lies in the quality of performance. Every black belt started at the very beginning!

THE CORRECT MIND AND BODY APPROACH IS NOT ONLY APPLICABLE IN THE DOJO, BUT EXTENDS TO THE COMPETITIVE ARENA TOO.

Grading system

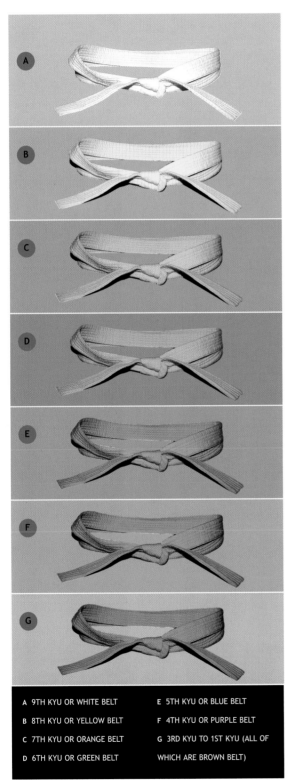

A 9TH KYU OR WHITE BELT

B 8TH KYU OR YELLOW BELT

C 7TH KYU OR ORANGE BELT

D 6TH KYU OR GREEN BELT

E 5TH KYU OR BLUE BELT

F 4TH KYU OR PURPLE BELT

G 3RD KYU TO 1ST KYU (ALL OF WHICH ARE BROWN BELT)

Each style of karate has its own grading syllabus, a way of measuring the performance and advancement of its students, and method of reward. The awarding of different colour belts is the accepted method of reward. A certain level of performance governs each grading. The higher the grading, the tougher the requirements and the greater the challenge for the karateka.

The belts

In certain styles, students are graded as follows, starting with the 9th *kyu* (step):

- 9th *kyu* (white belt)
- 8th *kyu* (yellow belt)
- 7th *kyu* (orange belt)
- 6th *kyu* (green belt)
- 5th *kyu* (blue belt)
- 4th *kyu* (purple belt)
- 3rd *kyu* (brown belt)
- 2nd *kyu* (brown belt)
- 1st *kyu* (brown belt)

From 1st *kyu* (brown belt), the student grades to 1st dan (black belt). This process can take up to three or four years to complete.

On reaching 1st dan, an entirely new challenge begins — but, of course, at a much more advanced level. From 1st dan, there may be a two-year training period before a student can grade for 2nd dan. From 2nd to 3rd dan would require approximately three years of training, and 4th dan four years, and so on. Some schools require the student to submit a thesis with each dan grading, showing the mental maturity and insight of the student at each higher level. It is therefore not unusual that a student grading for 4th dan, for instance, would need to be at least 30 years old to meet the intellectual requirements.

Some karate schools may award junior black belts to younger students (those under 18 years of age) without the theoretical component.

Gasshukus

A *gasshuku* is a training camp that offers a rather different backdrop and approach from the confines of a dojo. These camps may be presented in many ways: as a single day of rigorous training, a weekend of physical endurance, or even an entire week of intensive workout. What makes the *gasshuku* unique is that it is held outside the formal training environment where the students practise daily or weekly.

The training is tough and the terrain often rugged. The fine art of balance could be put to the test while practising kicks and punches on a tree log; the accuracy of performing particular stances could be measured while contending with the force of water in a stream or on the beach; and the mental and physical endurance may be matched against the rigours presented by the great outdoors.

A *gasshuku* is very hard work indeed, but it is also associated with a great deal of excitement and fun. Teamwork breeds team spirit and the great feeling of camaraderie allows the participants to leave the *gasshuku* filled with happy memories, sore muscles and a wonderful sense of achievement.

AT OUTDOOR TRAINING CAMPS, KNOWN AS *GASSHUKUS*, INTROSPECTION IS ENCOURAGED.

THE PHYSICAL AND PSYCHOLOGICAL ASPECTS OF KARATE ARE FUSED DURING OUTDOOR TRAINING CAMPS.

Understanding the masters

Many of the fundamental principles and techniques of the karate practised today were developed by the great masters who were instrumental in the growth of the latter-day martial art, popularizing it in modern society.

■ Widely recognized as the founder of modern karate, Gichin Funakoshi will be remembered for his simple, yet illuminating words: 'As a mirror's polished surface reflects whatever stands before it and a quiet valley carries even small sounds, so must the student of karate render his mind empty of selfishness and wickedness in an effort to react appropriately toward anything he might encounter. The ultimate aim of karate lies not in victory or defeat, but in the perfection of the character of the participant. This is the meaning of karate'.

■ One of the great Shotokan exponents who played a prominent role in modern karate is *Sensei* Hirokazu Kanazawa. He has earned worldwide recognition for his discipline and devotion to the art. At the first All Japan Karate Championships held in 1957, he won all his fights — despite fighting with a broken hand.

■ Gogen Yamaguchi, once head of the Japanese Goju style, is acknowledged for his tremendous contribution to Goju-Ryu.

Reaping the rewards

Always remember that if you are in conflict with yourself, you cannot execute what you have learnt!

There is no doubt that, after winning an individual or team event, an athlete is overwhelmed by emotion, the joy of success, satisfaction and a sense of achievement. It is a tremendous feeling to be a winner! Victory is most often rewarded with a medal, trophy or prize and, in some countries, money. On a personal and professional level, being awarded national honours or selection to represent your region, province or country in local or international events is a personal triumph for the athlete. Rewards afford honour, status and recognition.

THE TEACHINGS OF THE MASTERS ENCOURAGE EMPHASIS ON MENTAL DISCIPLINE AND PHYSICAL ASPECTS.

TECHNICAL ELEMENTS

Karate training is based on fundamental rules of conduct and the exercise of pre-determined techniques. While some beginners have a natural flair and perform with ease and confidence, some need to be guided through a rigid step-by-step programme. Whether the movements come naturally or through rigorous practice, there are basic techniques that require accurate performance: warm-up without burnout, stretching without straining, breathing without fainting, and balancing without stumbling.

There are no short cuts in training. Although the practise of the basic technical elements may seem repetitive, time consuming and extremely elementary, these fundamental techniques are essential to success. Karate, like any other sport, is built on practice and patience — particularly if you intend participating competitively. Patience, determination and dedication are essential ingredients for success, in the *dojo* and in the competitive arena, and ultimately for yourself.

above IT IS IMPORTANT FOR SPARRING PARTNERS TO UNDERSTAND THAT KUMITE IS A JOINT EXERCISE OF KICKING, BLOCKING AND PUNCHING.

opposite TO PERFORM WITH CONFIDENCE DEMANDS A COMMITMENT TO A RIGID TRAINING PROGRAMME.

BAG TRAINING ALLOWS YOU TO EXPERIENCE THE FULL IMPACT OF THE APPLICATION OF A TECHNIQUE.

Legs and feet

The legs and feet are valuable weapons in the karate 'arsenal'. While the beginner is developing a strong and stable stance, kicking should initially be slow and methodical. The brain records each movement of every technique like a strip of film, with one movement leading directly into the next. Karate can only be effective if the technique is sound.

Effective kicks can only be launched from an unwavering position. As the body becomes accustomed to grounding itself with greater ease and surety, so front snap, side thrust, roundhouse, backward roundhouse and back-thrust kicks are launched with greater speed, power and precision.

Diligent practice and the application of *kime* (the focusing of concentration and power) make for accurately landed kicks.

Definite movements govern each and every stance, punch, block and kick, but it is the combination of these basic techniques in different sequences that will decide the fate of both attacker and defender. Beginners to karate who feel confident enough to use their hips to generate power, have good balance and coordination, and have practised the basic techniques to the satisfaction their *Sensei*, are introduced to combination techniques, which in turn introduces them to the art of free sparring.

Fists and punches

The human body is taught to recognize and develop its potential to 'defend if attacked', but the methodology of 'how to defend successfully' requires careful instruction. The basic knowledge of how to fold the hand into a proper fist and direct a focused punch provides the groundwork for a variety of punches, including the straight, lunge, and reverse punch. The same applies to various defensive movements, such as the rising, downward, forearm and inside forearm block.

Effective punching — which involves breathing, power and speed — ensures delivery of a punch to the target, while effective blocking — involving timing, focus and distancing — prevents an attack from reaching its target. Remember, however, that 'a block is only a block when the position is correct'.

Body and mind

The practice of karate requires the unification of both physical and psychological aspects. While the physical (fighting element) can be taught and mastered to perfection, the psychological aspect is considerably more difficult to develop and maintain — and yet the two go hand in hand.

Mental toughness, therefore, means not falling apart in the face of adversity, not being struck by panic or fear, and maintaining *hara*, the energy that encourages the growth of spirit and character within each individual.

WHEN USED CORRECTLY, THE ELBOW CAN BE A POWERFUL WEAPON.

A SERIOUS STUDENT OF KARATE MAY PRACTISE MEDITATION AS A MEANS OF CONNECTING MIND, BODY AND SPIRIT.

Warming up

Before you practise any sport, it is essential to perform the required preparatory and warm-up exercises. You will need to limber up the body's major muscles and joints, and prepare the mind for the physical activity the body is about to be put through.

Warm up your muscles with stretching exercises before you launch into a programme of physical action. Jogging on the spot or in a circle and cycling are just some warm-up techniques. The warm-up should not be exhaustive, but of sufficient momentum to increase the heart rate and stimulate the circulation of the blood.

Cooling down

The exercise programme or practice should be followed by a cooling-down session: breathing exercises will slow down the heart rate and calm the mind, and stretching exercises will help prevent muscles stiffening.

Sit-ups

For this movement, use your stomach muscles and not your neck muscles. It is important to keep your knees bent, with your back and neck held straight.

⇩ When lifting your back off the floor (a), try to avoid swinging your arms upwards as this action will cause the neck to jerk forwards and increase the risk of injury.

⇩ Keep your arms stationary at the shoulders or rest them loosely on your chest (b) when pulling your upper body into a hunched position. For a sit-up to be effective, it is not necessary to lift your upper body flush against the knees.

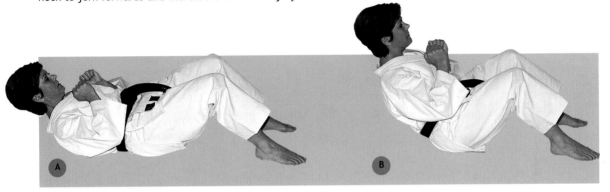

Press-ups

⇩ Lie face down on the floor, with your body fully extended and your back and buttocks in a straight line. Place your palms flat on the ground on either side of your shoulders.

⇩ Push upwards, using the strength in your arms. It is important not to let your body touch the floor as you lower your body on the downward thrust before you begin the upward thrust.

People who have lower back problems and may not have sufficient strength in their upper body to perform push-ups in which their weight is supported by the toes and fists, may lower their knees to the ground instead.

How to stretch

Correct technique involves a relaxed, sustained stretch with all your attention focused on the muscles you are working. If you stretch properly and regularly, the body will respond correctly to every movement required by karate. Incorrect stretching — all too common among the uninformed — involves simply bouncing up and down without purpose, or stretching to the point that the body experiences extreme pain. Incorrect stretching does more harm than good.

Easy stretches ⇩

Gradually ease your body into this stretch, spending 20–30 seconds in the position. When you reach the point of mild tension, relax while holding your body in position. The tension should gradually subside as the body becomes accustomed to the position. If not, ease the stretch slightly and find a degree of tension with which your body is comfortable.

Easy stretches reduce muscular tightness, and ready body tissue for advanced (static) stretches.

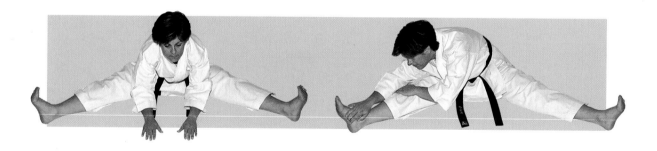

Static stretches ⇨

Once you have mastered easy stretches, you can gradually proceed to more advanced stretches by moving a fraction of an inch further down on each easy stretch. Do this until you feel mild tension in your body and hold the position for 20–30 seconds. If the tension persists, do not push your body; ease off slightly. Breathing should be slow and rhythmical. If you bend forwards to stretch, keep your back straight and breathe slowly while holding the stretch position. Do not hold your breath while stretching. If a position inhibits your breathing pattern, your body and mind are not relaxed enough.

Static stretches increase flexibility, promote circulation, increase the range of motion, reduce muscular tension, and prevent injuries.

⇦ ⇧   To avoid injury, movements that lead to leg stretches should be gradual and may need to be executed with the assistance of your partner.

Caution: *If you have suffered some form of physical injury, undergone surgery — particularly involving the joints and muscles — or there has been a period of inactivity, consult a physician before commencing a programme of physical exercise.*

Your body, the weapon

The realization that your body is, in fact, a 'walking weapon' may be rather startling. Hands, feet, knees, elbows, fingers, legs, as well as your head, take on a new meaning as the 'tools' of karate and the natural and always accessible weapons of attack and defence.

For your fingers, hands and feet to be effective as karate weapons, however, you will need a commitment from the entire body. Every effort should therefore be made to keep the body groomed, conditioned and trained to perform with coordination, power and speed.

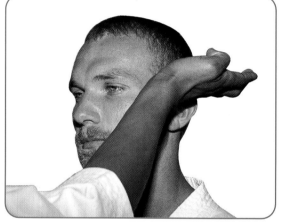

above THE SPEAR-HAND STRAIGHT THRUST (*NUKITE*).

right THE KNIFE-HAND STRIKE (*SHUTO-UCHI*).

below THE LUNGE PUNCH (*OI-ZUKI*) CENTRED ON THE LOWER FACE.

bottom THE LUNGE PUNCH (*OI-ZUKI*) CENTRED ON THE THROAT.

bottom right THE SIDEWAYS ELBOW STRIKE (*YOKO EMPI-UCHI*).

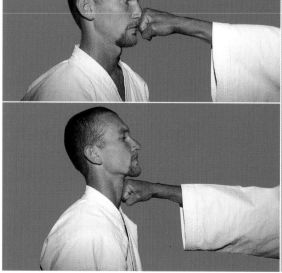

Your hands and feet

The hands and feet are the most widely used weapons in the performance of karate techniques. Attacking techniques, such as punches and kicks, often also serve as blocking techniques. The kicking leg (which, of course has a further distance to travel from the ground to the body target area on the opponent) can deliver three times as much power as the arm, while the supporting leg carries the full weight of the body. It is therefore necessary to develop strength in your legs and feet, which will in turn aid the speed at which the kick is executed.

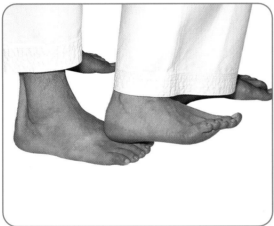

above THE ROUNDHOUSE KICK (*MAWASHI-GERI*).

left THE HEEL-OF-THE-FOOT STAMP DOWN.

bottom left THE BACKWARD ELBOW STRIKE (*USHIRO EMPI-UCHI*).

below THE BACK-OF-THE HEAD BUTT.

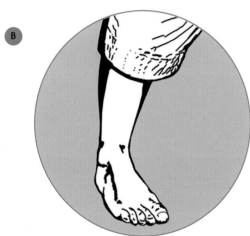

BODY PARTS MOST SUSCEPTIBLE TO INJURY ARE THE FACE, PARTI-
CULARLY THE NOSE (A) AND MOUTH, THE FEET (B) — MOST COMMON
IN KICKING MOVES — AND THE NECK AND LOWER BACK (C).

Injuries

Almost any sport exercise can cause injury:

- inappropriate or inadequate warm-ups
- faulty or excessive stretching
- the use of inappropriate equipment
- the application of faulty techniques
- performing inappropriate/excessive movements
- performing without adequate strength, stamina, suppleness, speed, coordination or endurance
- during inappropriate phases of relaxation/tension
- when using inappropriate muscles, ligaments, tendons during a performance
- psychological distress or exhaustion.

Common karate injuries

The most common injuries sustained in karate include:

- sprains (injury to ligaments)
- strains (injury to muscles or tendons)
- a bloody nose, cuts, bruises and scrapes
- blisters under the feet
- concussion
- unconsciousness.

Recommended treatment

- For sprains and strains the objective is to limit swelling. Remember the golden rule of 'RICE': rest, ice, compression and elevation.
- For a bloody nose the objective is to stop the bleeding. Sit down with knees bent, head placed between knees. Rest an ice-cold cloth on the nape of neck. Pinch the nostrils, without blowing the nose. Do not throw the head backwards to avoid swallowing blood, rather spit it out.
- For cuts, bruises and scrapes the objective is to stop the bleeding. Apply direct pressure. To cleanse and protect the wound, rinse adequately with a strong stream of clean water and treat with disinfectant. Be sure to use only sealed sterilized dressings such as band-aid strips, sterile gauze or protective padding.
- To treat blisters, open them and thoroughly cleanse the exposed area with disinfectant.
- In extreme cases seek medical attention.

Practical hints and training points

Overtraining can be just as detrimental to the body as undertraining. An overtired body can only deliver a mediocre performance. An overexhausted muscle can lead to an injury that can hamper both present and future performances.

Perfection lies in the quality of training and the education to a training timetable. To train for eight hours a day does not necessarily indicate super-fit status. Highly graded karate practitioners and successful champions are people who have made a decision to be disciplined and were disciplined enough to make that decision.

Remember: Sporadic training will inevitably lead to under-achievement, possibly even injury.

Practical reminders

■ Do not put force in your shoulders, but under them.

■ Without focus, or *kime* (see page 24) there is no true karate.

■ Do not take your eyes off your opponent as he will take advantage of any sign of weakness.

■ Quality is performance, not quantity.

■ Block with the body — the arms are accessories.

■ Add strength and speed to technique.

■ When performing *kata*, consider it the performance of a lifetime.

■ Maintain correct breathing in *kata* and *kumite* bouts.

■ Keep the mind strong.

■ Keep the spirit strong.

■ Work your karate from the inside — it cannot be understood from the outside looking in.

■ Always abide by the maxims of karate.

A LEG SWEEP (ASHI-BARAI), WHICH CONNECTS JUST ABOVE THE ANKLE, WILL DESTABILIZE AN OPPONENT DURING A KUMITE BOUT.

LEARNING THE BASICS

From the ready or fighting stance, you should be prepared to execute a series of punches, blocks, kicks — and the various combinations.

From the start

A strong and stable stance is the foundation of any karate technique. A technique — whether attacking or defensive — can only be effective if the body has both balance and stability in stance, mobility and flexibility in movement and a low centre of gravity. For a technique to be accurate, fast and powerful, it must therefore be launched from a stable base. (See page 48.)

It is from this basic position that punches, kicks and blocks are executed, so it is important that the novice *karateka* develop a sure-footed stance.

Punches

A punch comprises a fisted forearm that is thrust forward and targeted at the body of your opponent, while moving forwards from a standing position in an attack or defensive motion.

The part of the fist that makes contact with the target is the most important part of the hand. By using the base of the knuckles on the forefinger and middle finger, the focus of the force is more effective. Wrist, elbow, and shoulder perform a coordinated movement.

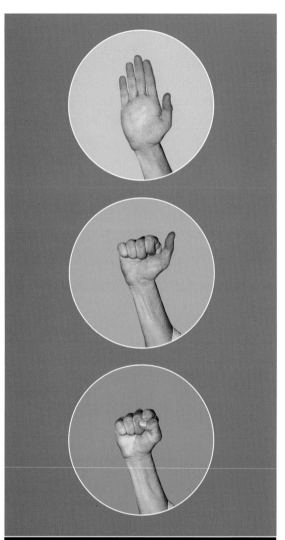

above STARTING WITH THE LITTLE FINGER, MAKE A FIST BY FOLDING THE FIRST FOUR FINGERS INTO THE PALM OF YOUR HAND AND LOCKING THE THUMB ACROSS THE INDEX AND MIDDLE FINGERS. KEEP THE FINGERS TIGHTLY CLENCHED. THE HAND SHOULD FORM A SOLID BLOCK, WHICH MAKES THE FORCE OF THE IMPACT MORE EFFECTIVE.
left MASTERING THE BASIC HAND POSITIONS WILL HELP IN THE DEVELOPMENT OF A SOUND FIGHTING STANCE.
opposite SIMPLE YET FUNDAMENTAL EXERCISES THAT STRENGTHEN THE WRIST AND HAND WILL ADD POWER TO YOUR PUNCH.

Straight punch (Choku-zuki)

 **A**

⇐ With your legs shoulder-width apart and your knees slightly bent (a), straighten both arms directly in front of you, with both hands clenched into fists, thumbs touching and fists pointing downwards.

 **B**

⇨ Relax the shoulders, with your hands slightly lower than shoulder level. Pull the right arm back to the side of the body so that it is in line with your ribs and above your hips. As you do this, turn the wrist so that it faces upward (b), and keep the elbow tucked in close to your body. Keep it there as your arm reaches out to execute a punch.

 **C**

⇐ Then, as the elbow of the right arm moves forward and away from your body, your wrist should turn downwards (c). The movements of both arms should correspond and be simultaneous and coordinated.

 **D**

⇨ As the right arm thrusts forward, pull the elbow of your left arm back sharply towards the side of the body and, as the left elbow arrives at your side, the wrist should automatically turn upwards (d).

> **Note:** The ready stance (yoi) shown in Figure A is the standard stance used for movements throughout this chapter.

Lunge punch (Oi-zuki) ⇩

Launching from a fighting stance, use your front foot to drive the rear foot forwards. At the same time, punch with the hand that corresponds to the forward foot so that your body moves into a forward stance. Throughout this movement, keep your hand at the side of the body and throw the punch only as your foot touches the floor in front of you.

When executing a lunge punch, keep the following in mind:

■ keep the body upright, with hips and shoulders locked forward
■ the hand pushes towards the centre of the opponent's body
■ keep the rear leg locked and the heel grounded.

The effectiveness of the punch lies in generating initial speed and maintaining power, to end with focus.

Make sure that the elbow of the punching arm moves flush against the side of your body as you lunge forwards to punch.

Reverse punch (Gyaku-zuki) ⇩

The reverse punch entails punching with the right arm as you step forwards with the left leg — or with the left arm as you step forwards with your right leg.

It is important that both hips extend forward in the direction of the target as you punch. To maintain your balance, keep your hips as low as possible.

The feet and knees remain grounded as your hips move. As with the *Oi-zuki* punch, the wrist must be kept firm and straight when performing the *Gyaku-zuki* punch, so that its impact is felt only on the two forefingers. Timing is critical. The reverse punch is a split second faster than the straight punch. This vertical punch is called *Tate zuki*.

The hips play a very important role in the execution of the reverse punch as they form the basis for the rotation of the upper body.

Blocks

The various blocks use the arm and hand as the prime 'weapons of defence'. A block should be executed the moment your opponent launches an attack on you.

Rising block (Age-uke) ↘

The rising block serves to defend the face area.

To perform the rising block, stand with your feet shoulder-width apart and your knees slightly bent. Hold your left arm straight in front of your body and pull your right arm to your side with the wrist turned upwards. As the right arm moves away from the body — keep it close to your side so that there is no swinging action outwards — the left arm moves towards the chest and is immediately followed by the right arm, which crosses on the outside. The right arm then continues the blocking action upwards with the forearm focusing approximately 15cm (6 inches) above and to the front of the head, with the inner wrist pointed away from the face. Simultaneously, the left arm pulls back to the side of the body so that it comes to rest at the same level as your lower rib. The strength of the rising block lies in the elbow.

When applying a block, it is advisable to shift the body forwards too, as this movement helps to break the force of the attack as the opponent's body lunges forwards.

⇧ The rising block, or *age-uke*, may also be executed with the left arm, as illustrated in the sideview here.

The left hand moves back in readiness for the counter-attack, while the eyes remain focused on the opponent's movements.

Downward block (Gedan-barai) ⇩

The downward block serves to protect the stomach and groin areas, while warding off an attack to the side of the body.

Stand with feet shoulder-width apart, your knees slightly bent and your left arm straight out in front of you. The right arm is pulled back to the right side of the body with your wrist turned upwards. With the underside of your wrist facing inward, pull your right hand up towards your left ear and your right elbow close to the chest.

Your right arm blocks downwards, moving diagonally across the body so that the point of focus is the upper thigh. As you reach the point of focus, the right fist — which should be pointing downward — should stop about 15cm (6 inches) above the upper thigh. At the same time, the left arm pulls back to the left side of the body and comes to rest at the bottom of your ribcage.

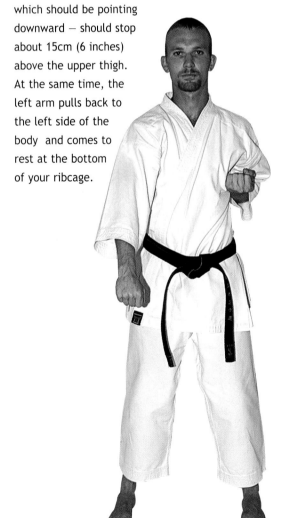

⇧ The downward block, or *gedan-barai*, may also be executed with the left arm, as illustrated in the sideview here.

Overblocking

Overblocking is as ineffective as under-blocking. To block effectively, focus the block at the hips. Swinging the arms beyond the hips and body would result in overblocking. This movement is not only a waste of energy, but will also have an adverse affect on your timing. Under-blocking, on the other hand, results in exposure of the ribs to your opponent in a counter-attack.

A block can only be considered effective if the entire body sustains the movement and supports the block.

Forearm block (Sozo ude-uke)

The forearm block serves to defend the torso, or upper body area, against attack.

⇩ Stand with feet shoulder-width apart and knees slightly bent. Your left arm should be held straight and extended forward in front of your body. The right arm is pulled back at the side of the body with the underside of your wrist turned upward. Pull the right hand up towards your right shoulder with the wrist facing forward and the elbow pressed against the body (a).

↻ The right arm then blocks in a semicircular sweep so that the wrist points towards your face at the moment it reaches the point of focus on your target. At this point, there should be a gap of about 15cm (6 inches) between your ribcage and the elbow of your right arm. Simultaneously, the left arm pulls back to the left side of your body and rests at the ribs (b).

⇩ The forearm block may also be executed with the left arm, as illustrated in the sideview here.

A   B

Following the wind-up, focus on turning the wrist sharply. This action will assist the lock of the forearm.

The strong, defensive movement with the forearm (known as the Ude-uke) is used to block an attack to the solar plexus.

Inside-forearm block (Uchi-uke)

The inside-forearm block defends the torso or upper body by deflecting the attack to the side.

⇓ Stand with feet shoulder-width apart and your legs slightly bent at the knees. The left arm is again straight and extended forward. The right arm is pulled back at the side of the body with the underside of your wrist turned upward. The right arm then moves across the chest, under the left arm and beyond the armpit with the wrist pointing downward (a).

⇗ Block your opponent with your forearm diagonally across the chest area with your wrist pointing upward so that the point of focus is at shoulder level. Again, there is about a 15cm (6-inch) gap between the ribcage and your right elbow. Simultaneously, the left arm pulls back to the left side of the body and lies alongside your ribs (b).

⇓ The inside-forearm block may also be executed with the left arm, as illustrated in the sideview here.

When executing the inside-forearm block, lock the elbow as you focus on the action of the wrist.

41

Kicks

While kicks are powerful attacks that can be quite destructive in comparison to punches and blocks, they tend to lack speed. To be effective, kicks need to be launched from a steady, strong and balanced stance and with as much force and speed as possible.

Lifting and bending the knee — with the foot held in a strong, controlled position — are important elements in the beginning stage of any kick.

An effective kick
To execute an effective kick, the supporting leg should remain rooted to the floor, while the knee is lifted up as high as possible, and the foot is pulled up as high as possible.

⇧ Kicks are executed from a fighting stance, with the left leg forward and left arm aligned to the left leg.

Front snap-kick (Mae geri keage)

⇨ From the fighting stance (see page 42), with the left leg forward and left arm aligned to left leg, lift the right knee up high towards your chest and pull your foot back, with your toes raised upwards (a).

⇩ Snap the foreleg out in front of you, kicking with the ball of the foot. Immediately after you have made contact with your target, snap the foot back sharply towards your body, with your knee still high up at chest level (b). Then place your foot back into the fighting stance, so that you are ready to proceed with a follow-up technique if necessary.

Through constant practice, the feet can become powerful and effective weapons. When kicking, pay special attention to the distribution of body weight. It is important that the leg executing the kick does not carry your full body weight.

Side-thrust kick (Yoko-geri-kekomi)

⇩ From a fighting stance (see page 42), lift the left knee high up towards the chest with the left foot pulled back and the toes raised at the same time (a). (It is important that body turn right simultaneously.)

The right foot remains grounded throughout the execution of this kick with the right leg slightly bent. When kicking, the upper body should be held as upright as possible. This ensures that the kick is executed with strength and from a balanced position.

⇗ Keeping your left knee raised, push your left hip up (b), but make sure that when performing the kick, your supporting leg turns to avoid injury to the knee.

⇩ Kick to the left, straightening and thrusting your leg so that the side of the foot lands on your opponent's body (c). The emphasis of the kick should be on the part of your foot that is strongest, usually towards the heel. On point of contact, pull the knee back high up towards your chest and then replace the foot in the starting position.

Back-thrust kick (Ushiro-geri-kekomi)

↘ Starting in the standard fighting position, with your right foot facing forward (a), spin clockwise on the ball of your right foot so that you have your back to your opponent.

↘ Once you have turned your back to your opponent, immediately lift your knee up towards your chest (b) and pull your foot up, with your toes raised back.

⇓ Thrust backwards with the right leg so that your heel makes contact with your target. Your toes should be pointing down-wards to avoid injury. Once you have made contact (c), snap your knee back and quickly turn your body in a clockwise position by putting your foot down so that you are facing your opponent again — your right leg should be facing forward — and your hands are up and in position to continue the attack on your opponent.

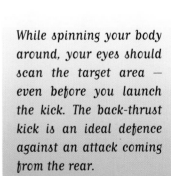

While spinning your body around, your eyes should scan the target area — even before you launch the kick. The back-thrust kick is an ideal defence against an attack coming from the rear.

Roundhouse kick (Mawashi-geri)

↘ From the fighting stance — with your left foot facing forward — raise your right knee high up to the side of the hip. The leg is folded in, the foot pulled back and the toes raised upwards to the same height as your knee.

Ⓐ

Ⓑ

⇐ Snap the leg towards the opponent (directly from your knee) with your foot pulled back so that it makes immediate contact with the opponent's target area — usually the temple or ribs.

After you have struck the target, snap the leg and hips back quickly and place the foot down in the fighting stance in which you started, ready to continue with the attack. Some styles use the instep and/or shin to strike the target.

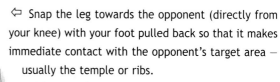

The higher the knee is pulled up, the higher the point of contact on your opponent's body.

Backward roundhouse kick
(Ushiro-mawashi-geri)

As with many other kicks, this manoeuvre can be executed with the heel of the foot and, as a result, can be very dangerous. It is not recommended for tournament karate, where kicking with the sole of the foot is far more appropriate.

It is much easier to perform the Ushiro-mawashi-geri if an opponent's left leg is facing forward. This is simply because an opponent's guard tends to be lower in the right arm than in the left, and not only reduces the chances of your being effectively blocked, but also increases your chances of landing on the target area.

⇨ From the fighting stance, pivot in a clockwise direction onto the left foot and hip (a), with your right knee bent and held up high and your leg folded back.

↘ Snap your leg out from the knee in a clockwise movement (b), making sure that the supporting leg is slightly bent.

⇩ After the sole (or heel) of the foot has impacted on the opponent's temple, face or neck, snap the leg and foot back sharply (c). It is important to snap the leg back quickly and place the foot back onto the ground (kicking leg facing forward) once you have completed the technique.

The stances

To ensure that karate techniques are performed with precision, it is important that you maintain the correct posture. When learning strong, stable stances, concentrate on your posture, with the upper body held firm and upright. Stepping forwards or backwards, sliding across the floor or turning can only be effective if executed from a position of stability. Remember, too, that shifting from one technique to another will inevitably increase the chance of losing balance – unless you are able to maintain the correct posture.

A strong stance

An important characteristic of a strong stance is that the back is held in an upright position, with your knees slightly bent, your feet firmly grounded, and your toes gripping the floor.

The ready stance (Yoi) ⇨

The ready stance is an alert position from which all training commences. Hold your chin up, with your eyes focused on your opponent. At no time should your chin drop to your chest. The feet should be facing foward, about shoulder-width apart, knees slightly bent so that the body is flexible enough for immediate acceleration. Your hands should be clenched in a fist, with the underside of the wrists pointing downwards toward the body and in line with the legs.

To measure the correct depth (in other words, the distance between your front and back leg) of the kamae, drop your back knee to the ground. It should be almost in line with the heel of your front foot, at a distance that corresponds to the height of your torso, or upper body area.

Fighting stance (Kamae)

The fighting stance, or *kamae*, is the position most commonly used in sparring.

From the fighting stance, not only are your hands and feet in a comfortable position to execute combination techniques, but shifting your body position and accelerated movements are easily executed when the feet are facing forward in the direction in which the body needs to move.

A

⇩ From the ready-stance position (chin up, feet facing forward and knees slightly bent), the left arm bends underneath the right arm while the right arm straightens to the front, elbows almost touching. As the left arm pulls across the chest in a blocking action, the right hand pulls back towards the solar plexus and the left leg moves forward into a fighting stance. It is important to note that the right hand does not pull back as far as the ribcage (as it would when you are throwing a punch).

⇩ Both fists, underside of the wrists pointing upwards, face the opponent. The left hand is in line with and at the same height as the left shoulder. Your legs should be shoulder-width apart, with the front knee bent over and in line with the front foot. Your back leg is straight and the hip pulled back at a 45° angle. The feet move in the direction in which the body is facing, with both arms in position and the hip pulled back, reducing your target area. Hips are kept low to enable you to accelerate forwards and backwards with ease.

⇦ Forward stance (Zenkutsu-dachi)

The forward stance, very similar to the fighting stance, differs only in that it is deeper and that the hand at your side is pulled further back towards the ribcage when applying a technique. This stance is ideal when you need to apply power and technique in a forward-moving direction. When moving forwards from the fighting stance to the forward stance, your knee should be bent over and in line with the front foot. Your back leg should be locked. Both feet face forward in the direction in which the body is pointing. Again, the hipline is placed low. In the blocking action, the hip will pull back at a 45° angle as the hand is pulled back towards the ribcage.

Powerful technique and a sound stance go hand in hand. The forward stance is well suited to rapid forward movement as the body is naturally positioned to move forwards.

⇧ The forward stance differs from the standard fighting stance in that it requires that you pull your right hand far back towards your ribs.

Straddle-leg stance (Kiba-dachi) ⇨

The straddle-leg stance resembles that of a rider sitting on horseback. The heels of both feet are in line, knees bent forward and outward, and hips lowered so that they face forward. Your full body weight is distributed directly above the centre of both legs. This stance — which encourages the development of strong legs, hips and ankles — is effective when dealing with attacks from more than one opponent and launched simultaneously to both sides of the body.

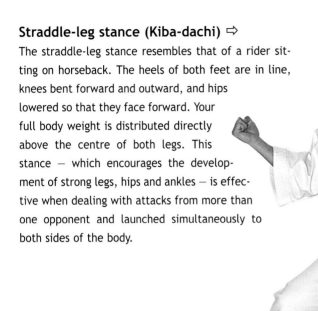

⇦ Back stance (Kokutsu-dachi)

From the ready stance, place the right foot forward and in line with the heel of the left foot, which simultaneously turns to the left as you move forwards. When performing this defensive stance, the back leg carries 70 per cent of the body weight. Both knees should be in line with the feet. Again, the hip is lowered. The back stance enables you to move your body beyond the reach of an attacker.

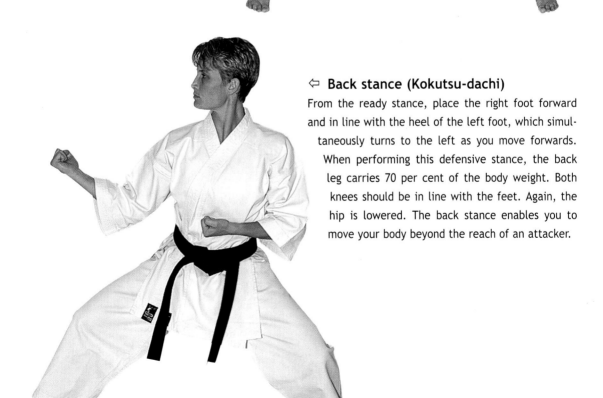

Basic technique combinations

Once the karateka feels confident and comfortable with the basic stances, blocks, punches and kicks, practising different combinations offers a new challenge. It is only with proficiency in each individual movement that the karateka is able to develop a 'follow-up' flow in the application of techniques.

The practice of combination techniques encourages the body to move naturally and respond automatically, which is especially important for free sparring (*kumite*).

↘ The attacker (right) steps in to punch the opponent's chest. In his own defence, the opponent (left) then slides backwards (a).

⇐ The attacker then punches a reverse punch with the left arm (b) and the opponent steps back, blocking the punch with his left arm.

⇐ The attacker follows up with a *mawashi-geri* kick (c) to the side of the opponent's face.

Aligning the hips ⇩

Effective karate techniques depend on power. Power, in turn, relies on the strong movement of the lower abdomen and hips.

When punching, keep your upper body upright because leaning forward could cause the hips to twist slightly — a movement that could lead to a weaker punch.

Hip movements ⇩

The movement of the hips plays an important role in the generation of power:

- to punch or kick, the hips rotate from a level position into a smooth and swift pushing action
- to perform a block, the hip is pulled back at a 45° angle, reducing the target area on the body
- to counterattack with a punch, the hips turn forward to conduct power through the body and into the punch.

Balance and coordination

Good balance and coordination form the foundation of karate because they are the basis for the application of all techniques.

Maintaining balance

Balance is the state of equilibrium maintained by the body, whether it is while executing a flying kick or during a stationary position in the execution of a stance. The coordination and synchronization of your movements, coupled with correct breathing, concentration and unwavering centre of gravity, combine to provide good balance while you move your body from one position to the next.

Tighten the lower abdominal muscles while keeping the upper part of your body straight and upright. The lower the centre of gravity, the greater the stability and balance. When kicking, the heel of the supporting foot must rest firmly on the floor. If the foot is slightly raised when kicking, your balance will falter.

JUMPING OVER A STICK IS A GOOD EXERCISE IN BALANCE AND REFLEX, CRITICAL ELEMENTS WHEN EXECUTING A TECHNIQUE IN MID-AIR.

⇧ When you are moving either forwards or backwards, be sure to keep the abdominal muscles tightened. Poor balance leads to bad timing and also reduces power in the performance.

⇧ Even with the reduced balance of just one foot grounded, the pool of energy is concentrated in the centre of the body, with the full body weight resting on just one foot.

Hara

In traditional martial arts, *hara* is the Japanese term for the lower abdomen, generally considered the 'seat of life'. It combines mind and body, and promotes the development of spirit and character. It is the spiritual essence that is responsible for maintaining calm, exercising self-control and enhancing awareness.

Ki (Life source)

The *karateka* can learn and develop technical skills, but these will not necessarily be effective if he is easily intimidated, is stressed or lacks confidence. Spirit is thus integral to karate. The Japanese call this central point the *ki*, which derives from the Chinese word *ch'i*, meaning the energy of all living things.

The 'physical centre' of this force is said to situated 5cm (2 inches) behind and below the navel. The development of *hara* or *ki* is linked to the practice of deep abdominal breathing.

Kiai (Spirited yell) ⇨

The word *kiai* is composed of *ki* (internal force) and *ai* (union), meaning the 'union of energy'. *Kiai* is the conscious use of a technique most of us have used at one time or another: like the grunt uttered when serving a tennis ball, or when pushing an extremely heavy object. The sound actually begins in the *hara*. Tensing the lower abdominal muscles while exhaling sharply results in *kiai*.

This 'spirited yell' is usually executed as the technique is focused.

- *Kiai* startles the opponent by breaking his or her concentration, affecting the return response and performance.
- It enhances the body's performance because exhaling tenses the stomach muscles, enabling it to absorb or buffer a blow from an opponent.

Kime (Focus)

The definition of *kime* in karate is the concentration of the body's energy in one explosive motion to a specific target area, using the appropriate technique with maximum power and speed. The relaxed muscles tense immediately at the moment of impact. *Kime* lasts for a split second and demands physical strength and mental coordination.

THE CONCENTRATED FORCE THAT HELPS TO STRENGTHEN THE STOMACH MUSCLES MAKES FOR A NATURAL *KIAI*.

Breathing

Breathing is the source of life. Training the body to breathe properly teaches the muscles to work together, ensuring that the diaphragm and abdominal muscles draw air into the lungs. Not all martial arts follow the same practices.

BREATHING EXERCISES THAT ARE PROPERLY PERFORMED HELP RELAX THE MUSCLES OF THE BODY PRIOR TO TRAINING.

Breathing properly

Proper breathing helps to:
- relax the body
- alleviate tension
- calm the mind
- promote the powerful performance of techniques
- promote spinal alignment
- establish a flow of communication between mind and body
- heighten both respiratory efficiency and metabolic activity of the body
- promote spiritual wellbeing.

Breathing exercises

Inhale through the nose or mouth and exhale through the mouth — slowly, evenly and with control. Use your diaphragm and stomach muscles (deep abdominal breathing) to draw air into the lungs. When inhaling, allow the abdomen to expand downwards and outwards, drawing air into the base of the lungs. Remain relaxed and do not allow the shoulders or chest to rise. Exhalation should feel like a release of tension.

ONE COMMON BREATHING EXERCISE INVOLVES DEEP BREATHING WHILE SITTING IN A RELAXED, UPRIGHT POSITION, WITH YOUR LEGS CROSSED IN TRADITIONAL YOGA STYLE AND HANDS RELAXED AND RESTING ON YOUR INNER THIGHS.

Bag and pad training ⇩

Performing punches, strikes and kicks against a heavy punchbag or a training partner's handpads allows you to launch into techniques with full power and directed commitment. This training also conditions the body to withstand the impact of hard blows. However, when starting bag training, begin by hitting lightly to avoid injuring your hands and wrists.

When you are hitting the bag with force, be sure to hold the hand and wrist in the correct position. Impact on the wrist — which may then cause it to bend involuntarily — can lead to serious injury. Naturally, therefore, bag training is not a recommended training technique for young children, because their bones and joints may not be sufficiently developed to absorb such high levels of impact.

Sparring with handpads is excellent training for competitions, because it allows your training partner to move around while you are punching the pads. This gives you the opportunity to coordinate your hand and foot movements and heightens your reflexes.

Weight training

Weight training (also referred to as resistance training) uses various weights for training specific muscle groups to increase and improve physical strength in the arms and legs. The principal reason for this is that the body's muscles will only improve in size and strength if the demands made on them is increased from time to time and the muscles are exerted to the maximum.

A strong muscle can bear stress without tearing. On the other hand, if a muscle is not used, it becomes weaker and smaller. Weight training can also improve the speed at which movements are performed and enhances coordination. However, be sure to exercise caution — particularly in the early stages of training — and apply the principle of progressive resistance: muscles need to adapt gradually to increased demands.

Strength

Strength is the ability to apply force and overcome resistance. Its development is indispensable for success in the performance of sport karate.

- **Explosive strength** is the ability to expend energy in one explosive act (punch or kick).
- **Dynamic strength** is the strength of the muscles used to move or support body mass repeatedly over a given period of time. This is important in high-intensity efforts of between 30 seconds and three minutes.

USING WEIGHTS WHEN PRACTISING PUNCHES AIDS IN THE DEVELOPMENT OF ARM, HAND AND SHOULDER MUSCLES.

MUSCLE STRENGTH IS A KEY FACTOR IN THE EXECUTION OF CERTAIN MOVEMENTS, ESPECIALLY EXPLOSIVE KICKS OR FLYING LEAPS.

KATA AND KUMITE

To the spectator, the different *kata* (formal exercises) resemble rhythmic dances. To the *karateka*, every *kata* is a different sequence of stylized movements and controlled techniques performed in a set pattern where the participant is fighting off two or more imaginary opponents.

The purpose of *kata*

Without *kata*, karate would be just another means of fighting. *Kata* teaches a stylized form of fighting. Only a person trained in the martial arts — and karate in particular — can perform *kata*, a sequence of movements characterized by effectiveness and efficiency.

To perform the many *kata* variations with success requires arduous training and discipline. *Kata* is the essence of karate and an important element in the training of other martial arts.

Kata symbolism

Kata is directly linked to the elements, and different *karateka* may have different approaches that are traditionally linked to these elements.

■ The earth-performer is steadfast, rooted to creation, performing the *kata* with strength and intensity.

■ The wind-performer moves with grace, power, and an ease that is serene.

■ The fire-performer is passionate and breathes light and life into the performance of the *kata*, radiating a warm, genuine energy.

■ The water-performer is natural, with a movement that flows harmoniously.

The grading system

The performance of *kata* is integral to the grading system. Although not a prerequisite for novice gradings, intermediate and advanced grades are measured by the performance of their respective *katas*.

It is fascinating to watch the *kata* divisions performing at championship level. A heightened excitement and sense of anticipation permeate the air as contestants proceed into the arena — energy and determination written on their faces — to deliver a performance that reflects their preparedness and skill coupled with grace and agility. *Karateka* project an energy that seems to command awe from the spectators.

Judges' criteria

In *kata* tournaments, the performance of the participants is judged on:

■ a realistic demonstration of the meaning of *kata*
■ an understanding of the techniques used (*bunkai*)
■ timing, rhythm, speed, balance and focus (*kime*)
■ correct use of breathing as an aid to *kime*
■ focus of attention (*chakugan*) and concentration
■ correct stances (*tachi*) with proper tension in the legs, and feet positioned flat on the floor
■ proper tension in the abdomen (*hara*) and stable hips — the hips should not bob up and down
■ the correct form (*kihon*) of the style that is being demonstrated
■ attitude and aura
■ in team (unison) *kata*, synchronization should not rely on external cues.

The spiritual element

On a spiritual level, *kata* training not only connects the performer to the inner self, but also serves to unite mind and movement.

opposite HIGHLY ACCLAIMED SOUTH AFRICAN NATIONAL CHAMPION JEFFREY JACKSON (RIGHT) SPARS WITH PROVINCIAL CHAMPION SHANE LUCAS DURING A WORK-OUT ON THE BEACH.

Beginner's *kata*: *empi-kata*

The Funakoshi *empi-kata* is a *kihon* (basic drill) in a *kata* form, using the elbow as a weapon. As the *karate-ka* progresses, movements become more complex, aiding the development of specific skills in stances, basic blocking, punching, kicking and striking techniques, training for posture, coordination and speed.

A—C From the *yoi* position, focus to the right, wind up with your arm and move your right leg into a *kiba-dachi* stance while striking with your elbow.

D—E Focus to the left and step up with your right leg, placing both feet together with your knees bent. Wind up with the left arm and step into *kiba-dachi* stance with your left leg, while using your elbow to strike.

F—H Pull your left hand back while covering your body with the right elbow. Balancing on your right leg, step forwards with your left leg and strike at the jaw with your left elbow. Reapeat with the right leg and elbow.

I—J Step to the left with your left leg, and use your left elbow to strike under the jaw. Look over your right shoulder as you have also jabbed the attacker behind you with your right elbow. Move your right leg in the opposite direction and strike with your right elbow upwards, while looking over your left shoulder.

K—M Covering your body with your left elbow, pull your right leg up so your foot is above the left ankle. Step back with your right leg and strike with your right elbow. With your right foot leading, turn to face the opposite direction and strike with your left elbow.

N—P Step forwards with the left leg while striking at the attacker's temple with your right elbow. Wind up with your right arm and strike the attacker's back.

Q—R Turn anti-clockwise on your left leg, so your right foot is above the left ankle. Extend arms and step back with the right leg; strike backwards with elbows.

S—U In a forward stance with elbows aligned under the jaw, wind up and strike downwards with the elbows.

V—Y Keeping your elbows in this position, step forwards with your right leg. Step up with your left leg, keeping your left foot just above the right ankle while crossing one arm over the other. Step into *kiba-dachi* stance with the left leg while striking with both elbows to the sides. Move back into the starting *yoi* position.

Understanding *kumite*

Unlike *kata*, kumite (fighting) involves the participation of a real opponent in a bout of free sparring. *Kumite* requires physical strength and raises physical as well as spiritual strength.

For the beginner, *kumite* should not be a series of random attacks and defences, but pre-arranged performances (preferably to the count of the *Sensei*) to ensure that techniques are executed with understanding and precision.

Kumite for intermediate grades

For the intermediate grades, semi-free sparring can be introduced. This allows for spontaneous movement, without prompting from the *Sensei*. Various combination techniques are introduced: for example, a roundhouse kick to the head, followed by a backfist strike to the side of the opponent's face, and ending with a punch to the body.

Advanced students practise freestyle sparring. Here the body is in a perpetual motion, defending and attacking or counter-attacking.

The practice of *kumite*

Kumite helps develop the following skills and abilities:
- enhances the ability to measure correct fighting distances
- promotes good attitude and form
- develops strong spirit and *kiai*
- exercises good timing, movement and control.

Kumite is not only about mastering the ability to control a potentially lethal blow or kick to defeat an opponent; it also fosters dignity, courage, strength of character and self-control.

TO SPAR SUCCESSFULLY WITH A PARTNER, YOU WILL NEED TO MASTER BOTH THE ATTACK AND DEFENCE MOVEMENTS.

Sparring with a partner

Sparring teaches you to develop your powers of obser-
vation. Being alert enables you to anticipate and identify the pattern of attack and defence — with you as
the attacker and your opponent as the defender.

⇧ A backward roundhouse kick (*ushiro-mawashi-geri*) is executed (a) against an opponent.

⇧ The opponent attempts to block (b) with a
back-thrust kick (*ushiro-geri-kekomi*).

⇧ A back-thrust kick (*ushiro-geri-kekomi*) is
launched (a) against an opponent.

⇧ The opponent may respond with a roundhouse kick (*mawashi-geri*) to the head (b).

SPORT KARATE

Some karate schools do not encourage karate as a competitive sport, because they feel that it should only be practised in a controlled manner, in keeping with its ancient Eastern philosophy.

Competitive karate

In recent years, *karateka* have recognized sport karate as an opportunity to meet new challenges and measure achievement. Sport karate has grown in popularity and has been instrumental in marketing and promoting the sport worldwide.

Competition offers the thrill of making it to the top and claiming the winning prize. There is no reason why karate, when practised as a sport, should not retain the traditional values of *budo* (the way of the warrior) while incorporating the challenge of healthy competition. The fundamental principles of respect towards others, a noble manner, virtuous conduct and self-control merely shift to the competitive arena.

Successful competitors share the thrill of achievement with their *Sensei* as well as officials involved in the preparation for and judging of a competition.

Sport karate has an appeal that draws many youngsters to the world of martial arts; initially, perhaps, to watch their heroes and later as competitors themselves.

For karate practitioners, competitive karate:

- is the meeting ground of fellow athletes
- is the learning ground for fellow athletes
- develops character
- encourages self-achievement
- encourages team spirit
- is the 'place of shared passion'.

ENTHUSIASTIC PARTICIPANTS IN THE SPORT MAY, WITH DEDICATION AND PERSEVERANCE, PROGRESS TO INTERNATIONAL COMPETITION.

CHAMPIONSHIP EVENTS OFFER UNIQUE OPPORTUNITIES TO COMPETE IN THE INTERNATIONAL ARENA.

World Karate Federation

In 1960, an international body was established under the name of the World Union of Karate Organisations (WUKO). On 6 June 1985, WUKO was officially recognized by the International Olympic Committee (IOC). Four years later, WUKO had 120 international members, 90 officially recognized by the IOC.

In 1993, the Federation Mondiale de Karate (FMK/WKF) was formed in Algeria and became the new official karate body, absorbing WUKO. Although the organization continues to strive for representation at the Olympic Games, chances of success for the 2004 Athens Games are slim.

The WKF unifies many of the world's *karateka* who practise either sport karate or traditional karate, and it promotes friendly bonds among athletes worldwide. It coordinates karate activities throughout the world, establishes technical and operational rules, and organizes and controls international meetings.

The world federation also reaches decisions on matters arising between its members. As the body qualified to organize tournaments, the WKF has the exclusive rights to world karate championships.

It may also organize other international competitions, including traditional karate events, and determines the conditions of eligibility applicable to participants. Today, the WKF consists of 156 member countries, divided into five continental unions:

- European Karate Federation (EKF)
- Pan-American Karate Federation (PKF)
- Union of African Karate Federations (UFAK)
- Asia Karate Federation (AKF)
- Oceania Karate Federation (OKF).

The directing committee of the WKF comprises 21 individuals and an executive committee of seven representatives. The president has a six-year term of office, while other office bearers hold their positions for four years.

The first world championships under the auspices of the WUKO were held in Tokyo, Japan, in 1970, with 33 countries represented and 178 athletes participating in the event.

The world senior championships and junior championships are held every second year.

The International Women's Cup, held in France, and the Women's International Championships, held in Japan, are both sanctioned by the WKF. The winners of continental championships and the first eight places in the World Championships are invited to attend the World Games, sanctioned by the IOC.

Scoring points in competition

The awarding of points in a competitive bout — be it one point (*ippon*), two points (*nihon*) or three points (*sanbon*) — is determined by the successful execution of a technique, followed by a scoring technique.

⇧ A simple punch to the body will score only one point (*ippon*) unless it is followed by a scoring technique.

⇧ *Sanbon* (three points) is awarded for a *jodan* kick to the opponent's head.

⇧ *Sanbon* is awarded for leg-sweeping the opponent to the mat, followed by a scoring technique.

⇧ A sweep may be followed by a punch to the body of an opponent who has been taken down.

The tournaments

There are three principal types of tournaments in sport karate:

- non-contact
- semi-contact
- full-contact.

Non-contact karate

- In non-contact karate, contact with the face or body is not permissible under any circumstances.

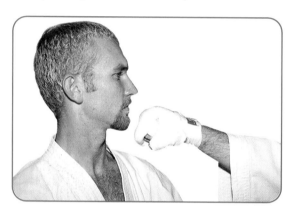

Semi-contact karate

- Hand or elbow strikes to the neck, back and head are not permitted.
- Kicks and strikes to the groin or breast area are not permitted.
- Semi-contact punches to the body are allowed.
- Semi-contact kicks to head and body are allowed.
- Kicks to the legs are not permitted.

Full-contact karate

- Hand or elbow strikes to the neck, back and head are not permitted.
- Kicks/strikes to groin or breast not permitted.
- Punches/elbow strikes to the body are allowed.
- Kicks to the head, body and legs — as well as sweeps to the legs — are allowed.
- Fighters may only grab the opponent's shoulder or the nape of the neck when executing knee kicks, sweeps or throwing techniques, but must then release the hold immediately after the move has been executed.

top NON-CONTACT KARATE ALLOWS NO CONTACT WITH THE OPPONENT.

above IN FULL-CONTACT KARATE, PUNCHES AND STRIKES ARE ALLOWED TO MAKE CONTACT WITH THE OPPONENT'S BODY.

WKF divisions

Rules at various tournaments may differ, but if the tournament is affiliated to the WKF, the federation's rules are strictly adhered to. Championships are divided into various WKF divisions:

- individual *kata*
- team *kata* (comprising three males or three females performing *kata* in unison)
- individual *kumite*
- team *kumite* (male teams comprise seven members, with five of these competing in a round; female teams comprise five members, three of whom compete in a round).

In a team event, it is the responsibility of the coach to identify the particular strengths of each of the participants and place them strategically in a performance order.

CAREFULLY CONTROLLED HIGH LEG SWEEPS ARE ACCEPTABLE IN FULL-CONTACT KARATE.

IN SEMI-CONTACT TOURNAMENTS, CONTROLLED SEMI-CONTACT PUNCHES TO THE BODY ARE PERMITTED.

The rules of competition

In standard *kata* and *kumite* competition, the fighting arena measures 8m² (25 sq ft), and should be level and empty. The panel for each *kumite* match comprises one referee, two judges and one arbitrator. A number of timekeepers and record keepers are also present.

The duration of a *kumite* bout is three minutes for senior males and two minutes for females. The referees and judges take up their prescribed positions on the mat. Following an exchange of bows between the participating contestants, the referee announces 'shobu hajime' and the bout then commences. When either of the contestants scores, the referee shouts 'yame' and orders them back to their starting lines while he returns to his. The point is awarded and the fight resumes. When a contestant has established a clear lead of eight points during a bout, the referee again calls 'yame' and the contestants return to their lines. The winner is declared and the referee, standing between the two contestants, indicates the victor by raising the hand closest to the winner, declaring 'shiro (white — or, occasionally, blue — belt) or aka (red belt) no kachi'. The bout ends at this point.

It is important that contestants remain alert even after the call of *yame*. One contestant may not have heard it above the peripheral noise that inevitably accompanies tournaments, or as a result of a deep level of concentration that shuts out activity beyond that of the fight. If a contestant has not heard the call, it could result in an unexpected kick or blow that could catch the contestant off guard and unprepared for further attack. This, in turn, could lead to serious injury for the unsuspecting contestant.

Neither contestant should, therefore, allow their concentration to lapse until they are absolutely sure that the fight has officially ended.

CONTESTANTS COMPETE ON PADDED MATS. REFEREES AND OFFICIALS ADJUDICATE FROM THE EDGES.

WHEN A CONTESTANT FALLS TO THE GROUND DURING A COMPETITION, A SCORE WILL BE AWARDED IF THAT CONTESTANT IS ABLE TO EFFECTIVELY LAUNCH AN ATTACK TO THE OPPONENT'S HEAD — A MOVE MOST EASILY EXECUTED WITH A SWIFT SWIPE OF THE FOOT.

Competition attire

Contestants in tournaments are required to wear a white, unmarked karate *gi* without stripes or piping. No jewellery or headbands may be worn and although a discreet hair clip is permitted in *kata*, hair slides and metal hair-grips are prohibited in a *kumite* match. Contestants must have short fingernails and women are permitted to wear a plain white T-shirt underneath their karate jackets. Protective boxes and soft shin-pads are allowed, while mitts and mouth-guards are compulsory. Shin-instep protectors are forbidden. Contestants are not permitted to wear glasses, but soft contact lenses may be worn. Women are allowed to wear authorized additional protective equipment, such as breast padding.

Scoring

Tournament judges award three points (*sanbon*), two points (*nihon*) and one point (*ippon*) according to:

- form
- awareness (*zanshin*)
- sporting attitude
- application
- timing
- distance.

Ippon is awarded for *chudan* (punches to the chest and stomach) or *jodan* (to the head) and *uchi* (strikes).

Sanbon is awarded for *jodan* kicks (to the head) and throwing or leg sweeping the opponent to the mat, followed by a scoring technique, such as a punch to the body.

The bout has ended with equal or no scores. The flag formation indicates a draw.

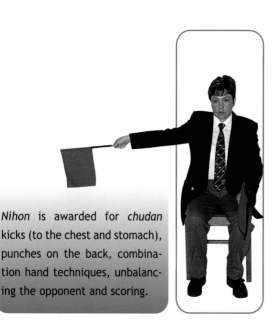

Nihon is awarded for *chudan* kicks (to the chest and stomach), punches on the back, combination hand techniques, unbalancing the opponent and scoring.

The bout

Attacks are limited to the head, face, neck, abdomen, chest, back and sides. The result of a bout is determined when a contestant obtains a clear lead of eight points, or the allotted three minutes have passed and one contestant has a distinct point advantage. One contestant may have a decision (*hantei*) against them, a *hansoku* (disqualified for making hard contact), *shikkaku* (disqualified from a bout, match or competition), or a *kiken* (renunciation) may imposed against the opponent.

When a bout ends with equal or no scores, the winner is decided by vote of the referee panel. The decision is based on the following:

- attitude
- fighting spirit
- strength
- tactics
- technique
- contestant initiating the majority of the action.

Prohibited behaviour

As with most competitive sports and especially martial arts, the behaviour of contestants in the competition area is restricted and regulated. Certain techniques and manoeuvres are forbidden:

- techniques that make excessive contact
- techniques that make contact with the throat
- attacks to arms or legs, groin, joints or instep
- attacks to the face with open-hand techniques
- dangerous throwing techniques that cause injury
- attacks with the head, knees or elbows
- repeated exits from the competition area
- self-endangerment (behaviour that exposes the contestant to injury by the opponent)
- techniques that, by their nature, cannot be controlled and jeopardize the safety of the opponent
- dangerous and uncontrolled attacks
- avoiding combat to prevent the opponent from scoring
- talking to or goading the opponent
- failing to obey the orders of the referee.
- discourteous behaviour towards the officials or other breaches of etiquette
- unnecessary clinching, wrestling, pushing or seizing without attempting a striking technique
- grabbing and attempting to throw or take down the opponent without making a genuine attack — except when the opponent attempts to grab or throw first
- throwing where the pivotal point is above hip level.

ALTHOUGH TECHNICAL MOVES, SUCH AS THE AXE KICK, ARE PERMITTED AND ARE INDEED FREQUENTLY SEEN IN THE COMPETITIVE ARENA, THEY ARE DIFFICULT TO EXECUTE AND COULD RESULT IN INJURY — AND POINTS — FOR THE OPPONENT IF NOT PERFORMED WITH CONTROL.

Understanding the terms

Penalty terminology

Keikoku	Warning with *Ippon* penalty
Hansoku-chui	Warning with *Nihon* penalty
Hansoku	Disqualification

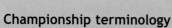

Championship terminology

The following terms are applicable to the scoring and refereeing of karate tournaments:

Ai-uchi	Simultaneous scoring techniques	*Keikoku*	Warning with *ippon* penalty
Aka	Red-belt contestant in *kumite*	*Kiken*	Renunciation
Aka (shiro) ippon	Red (white) scores one point	*Mienai*	Signal given by judges if they are
Aka (shiro) nihon	Red (white) scores two points		unsure that the technique reached
Aka (shiro) no kachi	Red (white) wins		a scoring area
Aka (shiro) sanbon	Red (white) scores three points	*Moto-no-ichi*	Original position
Atoshi-baraku	A little more time left	*Mubobi*	Self endangerment
Chukoku	First Category 1 or Category 2	*Nihon*	Two points
	warning without penalty	*Otagai-ni-rei*	Bow to each other
Encho	Prolonging match time	*Sanbon*	Three points
Encho-sen	Final extension of time	*Shikkaku*	Disqualification from a bout,
Fukushin	Judges		match and competition for a
Fukushin-shugo	Calling the judges together		serious breach of karate rules
Hajime	Begin or commence		and/or regulations
Hansoku	Disqualification	*Shiro*	White-belt contestant
Hansoku-chui	Warning with *nihon* penalty	*Shobu Hajime*	Start the match or bout
Hantei	Decision	*Shomen-ni-rei*	Bow to the front
Hikiwake	Draw	*Shugo*	Judges called
Ippon	One point	*Shushin*	Referees
Jikan	Take time	*Torimasen*	Unacceptable as scoring technique
Jogai	Exit from the match area	*Tsuzekete*	Fight on
Jogai-chui	Warning for leaving match area	*Tsuzukete Hajime*	Resume fighting or begin
Kansa	Arbitrator	*Yame*	Stop

Choosing a coach

While gradings test the essential elements of karate, tournaments put these elements to the ultimate test in a competitive arena. Although different styles have different grading requirements, tournaments in which more than one style of karate is in competition apply only one set of rules.

If you wish to participate in sport karate, it is essential that you do so with the assistance of an experienced coach. Ensure that your coach is well acquainted with the technical mastery of all the techniques. An open and honest relationship between coach and athlete allows for a deep and meaningful level of communication.

The responsibility of a feasible training programme should be a shared one in which both parties are active participants. Training for a championship, the coach guides the athlete to excel in sport karate, and it is essential that they develop a strong partnership built on trust and mutual respect. In this way, the athlete will honour the coach and realize that teamwork is an important factor in success — especially in a competitive arena.

The athlete:

- trusts the coach
- participates voluntarily
- is committed
- is disciplined to follow the training programme
- is technically capable
- trains with confidence
- understands the rules
- maintains general fitness
- has a desire to achieve and succeed.

The coach:

- has the technical expertise
- has creative flair
- encourages and motivates
- is a strategist
- is familiar with tournament rules
- is a counsellor, leader, friend and confidant
- strives towards specific objectives.

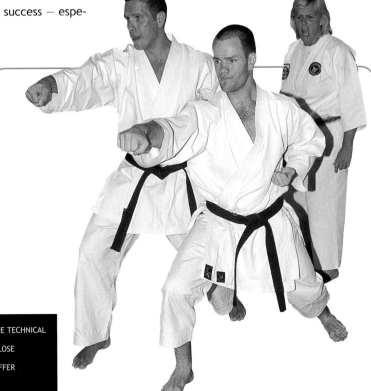

A COACH SHOULD NOT ONLY BE FAMILAR WITH THE TECHNICAL ELEMENTS OF KARATE, BUT ALSO HAVE BUILT A CLOSE ENOUGH RELATIONSHIP WITH THE STUDENT TO OFFER CONSTRUCTIVE ADVICE ON A SPIRITUAL LEVEL.

Preparing for tournaments

If you intend to be active in sport karate, try to obtain in advance all the tournament dates set out for the entire year. That way, your training programme can be planned accordingly. Mark the dates in the tournament calendar, and allocate enough training time before the tournament. This will enable sufficient peaking for specific championship events.

Basic training

A basic programme should be outlined — and followed — with attention to general fitness and stamina.

■ Karate is an anaerobic sport (go, stop, go, pause, go, stop), so a 5—10km (3—6 mile) jog is enough.

■ A regular 30-minute programme of circuit training in the gym should also enhance fitness.

■ Power training could include a 50m (165ft) uphill sprint, after which you walk back to the starting line. Remember to breathe evenly. This could be done at least 10 times at each training session.

■ Training for power, strength and speed can also be achieved by working out with weights in the gym.

Some karate athletes excel at speed, while others may not be quite as quick. For the athlete who is not particularly fast in the application of a technique, timing is an important element.

■ Prior to an event, a considerable amount of preparatory time should be spent on the *dojo* floor, sparring with a partner, practising combinations and take-down techniques, enhancing attack and escape strategies, and handpad training. As you prepare and condition your body to perform at a tournament, so should your mind be attuned to the challenges and pressures that go hand-in-hand with competitive performance. Positive thinking generates success.

Useful hint: Practice the art of visualization. Visualize yourself performing combination techniques and winning the bout at the forthcoming championship. This generates positive energy, and helps to set the goal — a positive step toward success and achievement.

TRAINING SHOULD INCLUDE EXERCISES THAT CONCENTRATE ON THE MUSCLES IN THE LIMBS, HANDS AND FEET IN ORDER TO TRAIN MUSCLE FIBRES USED IN EXPLOSIVE SPORTS SUCH AS KARATE, WHICH PLACE MUCH EMPHASIS ON ARM AND LEG MOVEMENT.

Tapering

Tapering (or winding down) prior to a championship event is very important and should be incorporated over a three- to 10-day period. This means that the athlete should train for three-minute bouts at a time, the same performance time required on the day of the competition. While it is important to maintain the intensity of workouts, you will need to reduce the amount of training prior to a tournament — because, at this point in your training regime, quality is more important than quantity.

Nutritional advice: carbo-load three days before the tournament by consuming pasta, bread, brown rice and potatoes. A carbohydrate meal or carbohydrate-rich fluids, such as energy drinks, taken two hours prior to the event will provide sufficient stamina to sustain the athlete during the competition.

Nutrition

During the tournament, drink high-carbohydrate fluids (rich in glucose). These have three principal benefits for the competitive athlete:

- preventing dehydration
- improving performance by maintaining blood glucose levels
- delaying fatigue when muscle glycogen stores are low or have been depleted.

After the competition, try to refuel on carbohydrates, including fluids, bread and fruit.

Recovery time

Unlike many other competitive sports, karate is not bound by the seasons, and competitive tournaments take place throughout the year. Competing in too many tournaments during the course of a year without replenishing the body's reserves with proper nutrition and allowing adequate time to recover from stress and injury can prove to be extremely taxing on the body of an athlete.

TRAINING PROGRAMMES SHOULD INCLUDE EXERCISES SUCH AS GENTLE JOGGING THAT HELP WIND THE BODY DOWN AFTER INTENSE ACTIVITY.

LIKE ALL SPORTS THAT DEMAND EXERTION OF THE BODY, A BALANCED DIET SHOULD INCLUDE RE-FUELLING CARBOHYDRATES SUCH AS FRUIT.

The fighters

Karate fighters fall into three different categories: some are technicians, some tacticians or defenders, and others attackers.

Technicians

Technicians are well-coordinated athletes who move naturally and effectively in the fighting arena. Their bodies are well positioned during a fight, with no movement in their hips at medium height. They execute swift body movements to the side, back and front and are good jumpers as well as sweepers. Fighters who use their hands and legs with confidence in combinations, perform the various karate techniques with ease.

It is often difficult to identify a technician's pattern of fighting as these fighters tend to use their hands and feet quickly and automatically.

⇧ The Technician (right) is able to execute sound combinations, which inevitably include jumps.

Tacticians

Tacticians (also known as defenders) concentrate on movements that rely on the back leg for effect, although throwing a punch remains a very popular manoeuvre. The tacticians' ability to block effectively counts in their favour. Body movements are direct and after executing a punch, they move back with speed to escape a blow. Tacticians move low on the hips and hold a close guard, waiting for the right moment to score. They are the ultimate strategists.

⇨ The low hips (right) are typical of a defender's stance.

THE LEG SWEEP (A) IS A TYPICAL TECHNIQUE IN THE ATTACK STYLE, AND WILL USUALLY BE FOLLOWED BY AN EQUALLY FAST PUNCH OR KICK (B) THAT RESULTS IN A SCORE.

Attackers

The attackers' style of fighting is characterized by the fact that they try to score valuable points at the beginning of the fight. Although they often tend to be emotional fighters, they are known to be strong and follow their own initiative.

The attacker's fight is conducted off the front leg with the hips held high. His guard is open and the footwork pushes forward. Attackers excel at executing both single and combination techniques and have the physical agility to move the body in different directions.

The opponent

Training against different kinds of fighters — be they technicians, tacticians or attackers — has a number of benefits for the *karateka*:

■ establishes a personal fighting style
■ assists in identifying the opponent's style in a tournament
■ teaches the fighter to adapt and be versatile.

The victor

To be a successful fighter, the *karateka*:

■ executes techniques with practicality, creativity, freedom and confidence
■ has the agility to move the body and follow up with combination techniques
■ should be adaptable, flexible and in harmony with him- or herself
■ must have a strong spirit
■ should know how and when to proceed.

SPEED AND AGILITY ARE IMPORTANT ELEMENTS WHEN DEFENDING AGAINST AN ATTACK IN ANY OF THE THREE FIGHTING STYLES.

KARATE AND SELF-DEFENCE

Karate is an extremely effective method of self-defence. The basics of karate establish a firm foundation for the training of useful self-defence techniques. *Kata* teaches the *karateka* to focus on physical and mental training and the perfection of technique, while the practice of *kumite* teaches the *karateka* to apply judgement and practise attack and defence. Some principles apply to both the karate athlete and the individual practising self-defence: the choice to attack or defend, the choice of technique or tool, and the choice to be the victim or the survivor.

Rules apply to karate tournaments as well as to dojo training, but there are no rules in a street attack! Kicking your opponent's groin in a championship is strictly prohibited, and kicking your fellow *karateka* in the groin when you are training or sparring in the *dojo* is considered disrespectful and indicates a lack of control. However, kicking your attacker in the groin when attacked in the street is good self-defence. No rules apply when a life is at risk — just the will to survive!

Practical self-defence

Practical and effective self-defence makes a number of demands on the potential victim. It requires:

- a mind shift
- mental and emotional strength
- physical form
- a competent performance
- a commitment to act with determination
- the need to succeed.

Attacks can come in many different forms. The reality is that attacks are often brutal and frightening, and a violation of personal space — but it need not lead to the unthinkable. The victim is bound to be hurt in some way or another, but the trick is to remain focused on the attacker, not on any injuries that may be sustained.

Effective self-defence

Effective self-defence does not rely on intricate techniques and formalized movements, but on the simple reactions. Both karate and general self-defence train the body to adopt a fighting stance, maintain adequate distance from the opponent, and develop a sense of timing. They also teach the individual to shift the body in defence and enhance awareness of impending danger. Not all people follow a martial art routine as a means of self-defence, but an effective punch to the correct target area can mean the difference between survival and defeat — and this is precisely what karate teaches from the outset: a straight punch (*choku-zuki*) is a blow struck with the fist in a straight line towards an imaginary attacker.

Making the mind shift

One of the most important factors in being able to defend yourself successfully is the ability to make the required mind shift that will allow you to be assertive and aggressively defensive. This is often particularly difficult for some women, many of whom may have been conditioned to be sensitive and nurturing and are unwilling to consciously hurt their attackers.

Karate training teaches the practitioner:

- to grasp the realities of confrontation
- to be strong when faced with real-life opponents
- the importance of regaining composure quickly when dealing with confrontational situations
- that techniques in isolation are only effective when executed with courage and conviction
- that part of making a mind shift includes turning a crisis into an opportunity!

opposite A POTENTIAL VICTIM WINDS UP TO STRIKE THE GROIN OF HER ATTACKER WITH HER ELBOW.

Body target areas

When you are attacked, you need to focus and figure out which sensitive body part of the attacker is available to hit, strike, poke or kick, and what part of your own body can be used as a weapon.

Some of the most sensitive target areas are the:

- face area, nose, jaw, throat, eyes, ears, temples
- side and back of the neck and hair
- solar plexus and ribs
- groin
- spine
- kneecaps, shin, and the bridge of the foot
- Achilles tendon
- the fingers and the top of the hand

The average man can, however, take a blow to the body, so it may be advisable to throw a punch, kick or elbow technique to the face or groin. Remember that attackers can be female too.

Principal self-defence weapons

Karate teaches you that the body is a weapon in its own right. The hands, fingers, elbows, knees, feet and head are tools in a time of crisis. If, for some reason, your body is restricted in an attack, try to improvise and use items from your immediate environment to your advantage: throw sand in your attacker's eyes if you are pinned down on the ground, grab a stick to ward off an assailant, or grab a vase, pen, set of car keys or any other accessible object that may be useful.

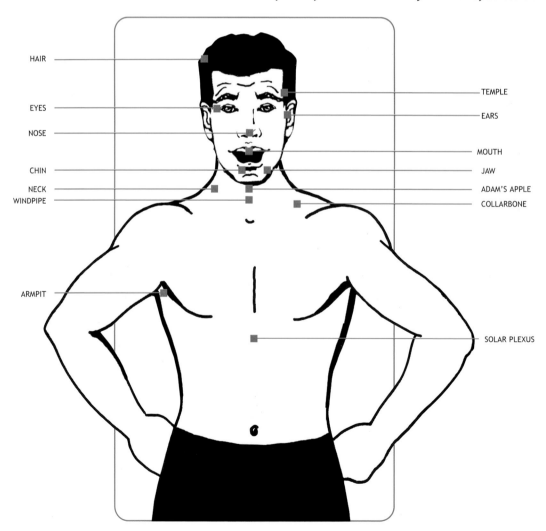

HAIR — EYES — NOSE — CHIN — NECK — WINDPIPE — ARMPIT

TEMPLE — EARS — MOUTH — JAW — ADAM'S APPLE — COLLARBONE — SOLAR PLEXUS

If you have been pushed up against a tree or wall, try not to focus on the fact that you have been incapacitated. Look for the advantages of being able to use the tree or wall in your favour, such as helping to maintain your balance. Launch your own attack from what is essentially a stable and secure position. If the attacker is within range, aim your kicks and punches at sensitive target areas, such as the neck, face or groin.

Making the commitment

In your commitment to succeed you need to eradicate fear and panic as quickly as possible. Fear and panic only serve to immobilize.

In an attack:

- stay as calm as possible
- be determined to succeed
- trust the decisions you have made
- follow through with the techniques
- do not give up and stay committed to the fight
- your intention must be to hurt the attacker
- get out of the situation as soon as possible.

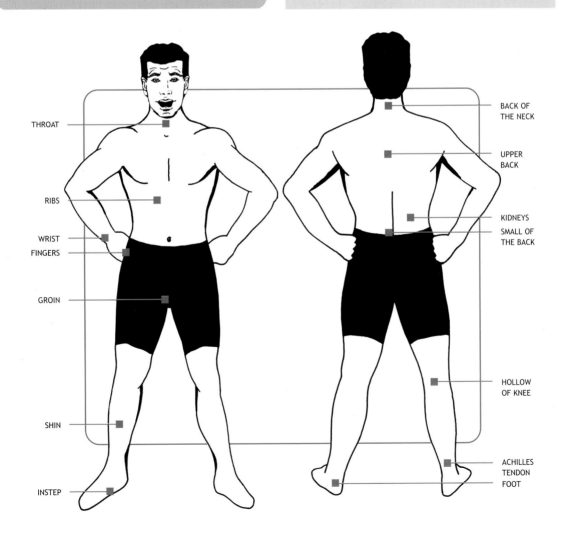

THROAT

RIBS

WRIST
FINGERS

GROIN

SHIN

INSTEP

BACK OF THE NECK

UPPER BACK

KIDNEYS
SMALL OF THE BACK

HOLLOW OF KNEE

ACHILLES TENDON
FOOT

Attack from the front

If at all possible, remember to shift your own body into a position that will facilitate your defence. This should help diffuse some of the attacker's body force on impact and create the correct distance needed for the counter-attack.

The attack

A The attacker tries to strangle you from the front, wrapping both hands around your throat.

B Wind up by cupping both hands, holding your fingers together and raising your arms so that your hands are at shoulder height. Using both hands, hit the attacker's ears simultaneously as if you were playing the cymbals. This can cause the eardrums to burst.

C Grab and hold onto the attacker's clothing while jabbing sharply into the groin with the knee. Grabbing the clothing will allow you to maintain your balance and will help you to direct the movement of your knee to the target.

The attack

The attacker grabs your throat with one hand and forces you against a tree or wall. If his nose, eyes, ears, throat or groin are within reach, try to strike any of these body target areas with as much force as you can muster.

A If your attacker's arms are so long that you cannot reach his face with ease and cannot execute a kick to the groin, insert two fingers between your throat and the attacker's thumb.

B Grab tightly onto his thumb, and bend it back sharply — with the intention of breaking it.

C While your hand grips the thumb, grab hold of the side of his arm with the other hand, twisting his arm in a clockwise direction so it is pulled to the back.

D Hold the attacker's arm out straight in this position.

E—F Raise your own arm as high as possible and bring your elbow down hard, using it as a weapon to strike down forcefully between his shoulder blades or even directly onto his spine.

The success of this technique lies in your commitment to pull the attacker's thumb backwards — with the full intent of breaking it. For the elbow to be effective, the arm has to be bent, allowing the elbow to function as an effective weapon with which to strike the target area with maximum power.

Attack from behind

The attack

A The attacker approaches from behind and grabs both arms in a bearhug grip. One option is to shift your hips to the side and hit downwards with your arm or hand into the attacker's groin or, alternatively, grab the groin and twist his testicles with force.

B Another option is to see where the attacker has placed his foot. Then lift your knee up high.

C Stamp down hard on the attacker's foot with the heel of your foot. He will inevitably loosen his grip.

D Drop your hips while shifting your legs into the straddle-leg stance *kiba-dachi* (see page 51), and block upwards with both arms.

E Quickly wind up with the elbow and hit any target areas on the assailant's body that may be open to attack: his face, solar plexus, or groin.

F If necessary, try to shift your body so that you are able to get your hand or arm down in order to strike the attacker's groin.

G—H As he folds over, break his nose with your knee, or strike your elbow down onto the back of his neck.

Attack from the side
The attack

A The attacker grabs you around the neck with one arm and locks his hands.

B Fling your arm up behind the attacker's back and over his shoulder. Place your strongest finger between his upper lip and his nose. Push and pull your hand backwards — hard enough so that he releases his grip.

C An alternative target area is the jaw. Hook your thumb underneath his jaw and, with a hard, focused push, shove his head sharply backward. Since you are not using both hands in this technique, one hand could effectivey strike the groin area.

The face is a very sensitive target area. When performing this technique, you could also stick your finger into the attacker's eyes or nostrils. Contrary to the general perception that it may be effective to push the attacker's jaw backwards, his neck muscles will probably be strong enough to counter this manoeuvre.

Attack on the ground
⇩ The attack

A The attacker is on his knees beside you and attempts to overpower you. One hand has a stranglehold around your kneck.

B Swing your leg up and hook it around his neck.

C Pull his head down to the ground, while lifting your body into a sitting position.

D Wind up high with your leg.

E Strike down with the heel of your foot on the attacker's nose or throat. If the kick fails, the attacker may try to grab at you. Try to snap and twist his fingers; the pain will be so intense that he will probably back off.

⇧ The attack

A You are attacked while lying on your back, or have been thrown to the ground by an attacker.

B Position your legs on the inside of the attacker's ankles and hook your feet around his legs.

C With a strong, focused action, push your feet apart and pull them towards your chest. This should unbalance your attacker and throw him over onto his back.

D Lift one leg up high and bring down the heel of your foot hard onto the attacker's groin.

MAKING CONTACT

INTERNATIONAL KARATE ASSOCIATIONS

AMERICAN AMATEUR KARATE FEDERATION (AAKF)

- 1930 Wilshire Blvd, Suite 1208, Los Angeles, CA 90057
- Tel: (213) 483 8262
- Fax: (213) 483 4060
- E-mail: aakf@aakf.org

BRITISH COLUMBIA KARATE (CANADA)

- 220–1367 West Broadway, Vancouver BC, V6H 4A9, Canada
- Tel: (604) 737 3051
- Fax: (604) 737 6043
- E-mail: info@karatebc.org

DENMARK KARATE ASSOCIATION

- Kasatnievej 20, DK–7470 Karup, Denmark
- Tel: (45) 9710 2482
- Fax: (45) 9710 0330
- E-mail: jka@jka.dk

ENGLISH KARATE GOVERNING BODY (EKGB)

- 53 Windmill Balk Lane, Doncaster, N. Yorks DN6 7SF, UK
- Tel: (1302) 33 7645
- Fax: (1302) 33 7645
- E-mail: info@ekgb.org.uk

EUROPEAN PROFESSIONAL KARATE ASSOCIATION

- Apartado Correos 6061, 48080 Bilbao, Spain
- Tel: (94) 441 6149
- E-mail: informacion@epka.org

FRENCH FEDERATION OF KARATE

- 122 Rue de la Tomobe, Issoire 75014, Paris, France
- Tel: (1) 43 95 42 00
- Fax: (1) 45 43 89 84

GERMAN KARATE ASSOCIATION

- Grabenstr. 37, 45964 Gladbeck, Germany
- Tel: (20) 4329 8800
- Fax: (20) 4329 8891

HELLENIC KARATE FEDERATION

- 149 Vizantiou Street, Kalogreza, Athens 14235, Greece
- Tel: (1) 271 7564
- Fax: (1) 271 7563
- E-mail: karate@ath.forthnet.gr

INTERNATIONAL TRADITIONAL KARATE ASSOCIATION

- 5945 W. Irving Park Road, Chicago, IL 60634, USA
- E-mail: info@itka-karate.com

ITALIAN FEDERATION OF KARATE

- 68-20137 Milano, Italy
- Tel: (2) 5990 0103
- E-mail: segretaria@fikta.it

JAPANESE KARATE ASSOCIATION

- 2-23-15 Koraku Bunkyo-Ku, Tokyo 112-0004, Japan
- Tel: (3) 5800 3091/5
- Fax: (3) 5800 3100

JAPANESE KARATE DO FEDERATION

- Nihon Zaidan Bldg 6F, 1-11-2 Toranomon, Minato-ku, Tokyo, Japan
- Tel: (3) 3503 6637
- Fax: (3) 3503 6638
- E-mail: jkf@blue.ocn.ne.jp

KARATE ASSOCIATION OF SOUTH AFRICA

- 55 Von Willigh Crescent, Kuils River 7580, Cape Town, South Africa
- Tel: (21) 903 7537
- E-mail: lbeech@atc.wcape.school.za

KARATE NEW ZEALAND

- P.O. Box 1237, Whangarei, New Zealand
- Tel: 0800 367 527
- E-mail: bob@karatenz.co.nz

KARATE UNION OF AUSTRALIA

- 18 Odalberree Drive, Uranga, NSW 2455, Australia
- Tel: (02) 6655 5320
- E-mail: sfilet@midcoast.com.au

KARATE UNION OF GREAT BRITAIN

- P.O. Box 3, Wirral L43 6XX, UK
- Tel: (151) 652 1208

NORTHERN IRELAND KARATE ASSOCIATION

- 3rd Floor, 35 College Street, Belfast BT1 6BU, Ireland
- Tel: (1232) 61 6453

SCOTTISH KARATE BOARD

- 2 Strathdee Road, Netherlee, Glasgow G44 3TJ, Scotland
- Tel: (141) 633 1116

SPANISH FEDERATION OF KARATE

- C/Princesa 22, 28008 Madrid, Spain
- Tel: (91) 542 4625
- Tel: (91) 542 4913
- E-mail: fek@arrakis.es

UNION OF AFRICAN KARATE FEDERATIONS (UFAK)

- P.O. Box 324, Bruma 2026, South Africa
- Tel: (11) 6431 414
- Fax: (11) 643 1440
- E-mail: iabdulla@netactive.co.za

USA KARATE FEDERATION

- 1300 Kenmore Blvd, Akron, Ohio 44314, USA
- Tel: (330) 753 3114
- Fax: (330) 753 6967
- E-mail: usakf@raex.com

WELSH KARATE FEDERATION

- Maes Hyfryd, Llanrug, Caernarfon, Gwynedd, LL55 4BE, UK
- Tel: (1286) 67 1912
- E-mail: gwyn@wtkf.co.uk

WORLD KARATE FEDERATION

- 122 Rue de la Tomobe, Issoire 75014, Paris, France
- Tel: (1) 43 95 42 00
- Fax: (1) 45 43 89 84
- E-mail: secretariat@wkf.net

WORLD UNION OF KARATE ORGANIZATIONS

- Senpaku Sinko Building, 1-15-16 Toranoman, Minato-ku, Tokyo 105, Japan
- Tel: (3) 503 6638

GLOSSARY

Age-uke	Rising block
Ashi-barai	Leg (ankle) sweep
Bu	Martial
Budo	The martial way or path
Bunkai	Kata applications
Bushido	The way of the warrior (moral ethic code)
Chudan	Middle level (the stomach)
Choku-zuki	Straight punch
Dan	Black-belt grade (degree)
Dojo	Training hall, or 'place of the way'
Empi	Elbow
Empi-uchi	Elbow strike
Fumikomi	Stamp kick (crushing the foot)
Fumitsuki	Stamping down
Gasshuku	Special training camp often conducted in the outdoors
Gedan	Lower level (the groin)
Gedan-barai	Downward block
-Geri	Kick (combinations)
Gi	Training suit
Go	Hard
Godan	5th dan
Gyaku-zuki	Reverse punch
Hai	Yes
Haito	Ridge hand
Haito-uchi	Ridge-hand strike
Hara	The spiritual centre located in the abdominal area. The source of *ki*.
Hiraken	Foreknuckle fist
Honbu	Main *dojo* or headquarters
Ippon-shobu	Full-point contest
Jiyu-ippon kumite	Semi-free one-step sparring
Jiyu-kumite	Free sparring
Jodan	Upper level (the face)
Jodan-zuki	Front punch to the head area
Ka	Person or practitioner
Kakato-geri	A kick with the heel
Kamae	Fighting stance; on guard
Karate	Empty hand
Kata	Fixed sequence of training exercises that incorporate aspects of attack and defence and takes the form of fighting with an imaginary opponent
Keage	Snap kick
Kekomi	A thrusting kick
Ki	Spirit, inner power, or life force
Kiai	Spirited shout
Kiba-dachi	Straddle-leg stance
Kihon	The basic technical forms of training and fighting
Kime	Focus
Kokutsu-dachi	Back stance
Kumite	Sparring
Kyu	Lower grade, the rank below black belt
Yondan	4th dan
Mae-geri	Front kick
Mae-geri-kekomi	Front-thrust kick
Makiwara	A padded board for punching and kicking exercises
Mawashi-geri	Roundhouse kick
Mawashi-zuki	Roundhouse punch
Mawate	Turn
Nage-waza	Throwing techniques
Nidan	2nd dan
Nidan-geri	Double kick
Nukite	Spear hand
Obi	Belt
Oi-zuki	Lunge punch; stepping punch
Osu	'Yes, I understand'
Rei	Command to bow
Ren-zuki	Combination punching
Sandan	3rd Dan
Satori	Enlightenment, ultimate knowledge
Seiken	Forefist
Sempai	Senior
Sensei	Teacher
Shihan	Master, honourable professor
Shodan	1st dan
Shuto	Knife or sword hand
Shuto-uchi	Knife- or sword-hand strike
Tatami	Woven straw mats

Teisho	Palm heel		Yoko-geri-kekomi	Side-thrust kick
Tsuki (or Zuki)	Punch		Zanshin	State of calm concentration, continued commitment, and alertness at the moment of attack or defence.
Ude	Arm			
Uke	Block			
Uchi	Strike		Zenkutsu-dachi	Forward stance
Uchi-uke	Outside-forearm block		Zuki (or Tsuki)	Punch
Ude-uke	Inside-forearm block			
Uraken-uchi	Back-fist strike			

Numerals

Ushiro-geri	Back kick		Ichi	1	One
Ushiro-geri-keage	Back-snap kick		Ni	2	Two
Ushiro-geri-kekomi	Back-thrust kick		San	3	Three
Ushiro-mawashi-geri	Back-roundhouse kick		Shi	4	Four
Waza	Techniques or skills		Go	5	Five
Yame	Stop or halt		Roku	6	Six
Yoi	Get ready		Shichi	7	Seven
Yoko	Side		Hachi	8	Eight
Yoko-geri	Side kick		Ku	9	Nine
Yoko-geri-keage	Side-snap kick		Ju	10	Ten

DEVOTED KARATEKA APPRECIATE THE DISCIPLINE OF MIND, BODY AND SPIRIT ATTAINED THROUGH COMMITTED TRAINING.

INDEX

PHOTOGRAPHIC CREDITS

All photography by Pieter Smit, with the exception of the following photographs supplied by photographers and/or agencies (copyright rests with these individuals and/or their agencies):

6   Fran Hunziker

11   Tony Stone/Philip Lee Harvey

23   Gallo Images/Tony Stone/Christopher Bissell

25 (r) Ryno Reyneke/New Holland Image Library

57 (r) Ryno Reyneke/New Holland Image Library

59 (l) Jacques Marais/New Holland Image Library

66 (b) Fran Hunziker

67—68 Fran Hunziker

72   Fran Hunziker

79   Ryno Reyneke/New Holland Image Library